LAUGHING LAST

Alger Hiss by Tony Hiss

LAUGHING LAST

Alger Hiss by Tony Hiss

1977

HOUGHTON MIFFLIN COMPANY

Boston

Library of Congress Cataloging in Publication Data

Hiss, Anthony.
    Laughing last.

    1. Hiss, Alger.   2. United States. Department of State
— Officials and employees — Biography.   3. Communism
— United States — 1917–   I. Title.
E748.H59H57   364.1'31'0924   [B]   76-49940
ISBN 0-395-24899-X

Printed in the United States of America

v   10   9   8   7   6   5   4   3   2   1

Some things are so serious you have to laugh about them.

> — Niels Bohr explaining why some of his students, sitting in a room discussing the ultimate death of the universe, were laughing

Hiss went to jail but at least he's alive, selling stationery.

> — William Goldman in
> *Marathon Man*

Contents

LAUGHING LAST

Alger Hiss by Tony Hiss

1. How Do You Get a Name Like That, Anyway?

At the age of seventy-two, my dad, Alger Hiss, has never been happier in his life. He lives in New York with a lady friend in an apartment near Gramercy Park not far from where I live. Al practices a little law, services his accounts in the downtown printing and stationery concern he works for, takes naps, listens to classical music on the radio, goes for walks and sometimes to show-biz parties. He has a little house in East Hampton, Long Island. He's leading a pretty normal, ordinary life. He reads the *New York Times* every day he can get it, he wears wide ties, he watches tennis and the New York Mets on TV, he likes Italian food, he does some university lecturing, and he writes down the vintages and vineyards of bottles of wine he's enjoyed drinking in a notebook.

So why the hell is he happy? He was publicly branded a traitor almost thirty years ago. Many people still think of him as the Benedict Arnold of the twentieth century, and he's a convicted felon who spent forty-four months in federal prison for denying charges of Communist espionage. People who have an explanation for Al's behavior these days tend to see him either as an unregenerate old villain or a spotless martyr.

But I'm in a curious position and don't have to see him as saint or sinner. I'm his son, and in fact I like him a lot, but I'm also a reporter and have been trained to say what I see.

What I've seen and what I can tell about is what no one else has told before — the private life of a man whose public life has been so melodramatic that finding in it anything other than melodramatic motivations and revelations has become virtually impossible. Up to now people have had to try to explain what happened in public on the basis of what they guessed had happened in private. For instance, I have heard as "true stories" about Al that President Roosevelt wanted to help the Russians and secretly ordered dad to spy for them; that mom was a Russian spy and dad was covering up for her (this was Mrs. Roosevelt's own explanation); that Whittaker Chambers, the man who denounced dad as a Russian spy, was under Kremlin orders to frame dad and thereby discredit President Truman; that dad and Chambers were lovers (this is Dick Nixon's explanation); that Chambers and mom were lovers; that Chambers and my brother Tim were lovers; that dad allowed himself to be jailed so that no one would ever know that mom had had an abortion back in the 1920s or that Tim had been kicked out of the navy for a gay episode as a teen-ager in the 1940s.

The only fact here is that Al is a naturally private man, and so his private life has been the one piece of the puzzle that hasn't been available before. That is what I have to offer — and frankly it took me a while to persuade him this story is worth the telling. So this book will be of interest to anyone who thought there was something missing in anything they have read previously about Al. And this book invites you to make up your own mind about my pop, and presents a life, not a court case. From this point of view the public events — the court case — are part of a life, and I think anyone who reads this book through to the end will see that the court case

makes quite a different kind of sense. And the reasons that
Al can be happy, as the reader will discover, have nothing to
do with winning or losing. As Al himself says, "Forty-four
months in jail is a good corrective to three years at Harvard."

The first question that has to be asked about the life of a
man named Alger Hiss is obvious — how do you get a name
like that, anyway?

There are probably only a few hundred Hisses in the country. I know of Hisses in Baltimore, Florida, and Los Angeles,
where Dr. Hiss Shoes has been a successful store on the
Miracle Mile in downtown Beverly Hills for a number of
years. We are all products of Valentine Hiss, who arrived in
Baltimore on a boat from Europe in the 1760s. Baltimore had
a lot of Germans at the turn of this century, and the story
when Al was growing up there was that Valentine was a
Prussian connected to the princely family of Hesse-Darmstadt.
Mary C. Hiss, the family historian, an elderly maiden cousin
of Al's who died in Baltimore in 1975, later changed the
legend and made Valentine a Dutchman, a van Huys — *van*,
of course. Maybe he was Swiss. In Sweden the word "hiss"
means "elevator." In Mexico it means "piece of chalk."
There are some one-S Hises in Basel, and — here is the
third family theory of distinguished connections — a Dr.
Wilhelm His from Basel, who practiced in Leipzig in the
nineteenth century, created the science of histogenesis, the
study of the origin of different pieces of embryonic tissue. He
was once shown what was supposedly the skull of Johann
Sebastian Bach and figured out a way of determining whether
relics actually had been part of historical people. His son,
Wilhelm His, Jr., was an eminent cardiologist who discovered
the bundle of His, the fibers in the heart that transmit the
squeeze order from the atria to the ventricles. He also discovered His's band, His's disease, and His's spindle. We're
probably not related, but people in Baltimore used to like to

think about these things. The most notable Hiss today is Mike Hiss, a distant cousin of ours who drove in the Indy 500 last year and was rookie-of-the-year when he broke in as a professional racing car driver a few years ago. Al and his brother Donie, a customs lawyer who just retired from Covington & Burling, Dean Acheson's old law firm in Washington, both collect newspaper clips about Mike Hiss.

Great-uncle George Hiss, Al's uncle, who made a million in a cotton mill in North Carolina, told Al's older brother, Bosley, that the Hisses are Jews, like the Hesses who owned a big shoe store in Baltimore. But that was after Bosley had been boasting about the family one night, and the next morning George told Bosley, who hadn't slept a wink all night, that it wasn't true, we really are WASPs, although George said he'd be just as glad if it were true. Valentine Hiss had one son, Jacob. Jake had sixteen children, which is where what Hisses there are come from.

The early Hisses were chiefly remarkable for living to great ages and having lots of children. Jake lived to be seventy-seven and died when he was struck by lightning while standing at his pump. His oldest boy, Jesse Lee Hiss, lived to be eighty-eight and was named for the Virginia Methodist clergyman who got the nickname "Apostle of Methodism in New England." *His* oldest boy, George Millemon Hiss, married a Bosley, which gave the Hisses something to talk about because the Bosleys traced back to the *Ark* and the *Dove*, Lord Baltimore's two little ships which brought the first white men to Maryland. This explains why Alger had a brother named Bosley Hiss. But in defense of Hiss pretensions let me add that there is a small street in Baltimore called Hiss Avenue, and there's also a Hiss Methodist Church somewhere in Baltimore. The family wherewithal was substantially improved for several generations by income from the Beaver Dam Marble Quarry outside Baltimore. All the famous marble stoops of lower-middle-class Baltimore come from this marble, and another family legend has always maintained that the Washington Monument was entirely constructed of Beaver Dam marble. By the time Al was a small boy the quarry was full of water and good only for swimming. George M. Hiss, who was an architect and owned several large paper mills outside Baltimore, hung out with Russell Alexander Alger, an Ohioan who made a fortune in the lumber business in Michigan and rose from the ranks in the Civil War to become a major general, so George named his third boy, born in 1864, Charles Alger. Charles Alger, my granddad, named his second son, born November 11, 1904, Alger in order to prove to himself that he didn't have a grudge against his father, George. What had happened was that after the Civil War Russell A. Alger went into politics and became McKinley's secretary of war just in time to take the rap for bad planning in the Spanish-American War of 1898, in which year the word "Algerism" was coined as a synonym for bungling inefficiency. Charles Alger couldn't prove anything directly to his dad because George Millemon had died in 1886.

Charles Alger was a pleasant-looking guy with big ears and a mustache who went into the dry goods business and ran the notions department for Daniel Miller & Company, one of the biggest outfits in Baltimore. He married Mary Lavinia Hughes, my grandma, a tough old battle-axe who was born in 1868 and died in 1958. Grandma once bought a ruled notebook in which she wrote down five pages of her own ancestry, a popular Baltimore pastime, and recorded her own children's birthdays — getting Alger's wrong by a year. I got the notebook last year after Mary C.'s death, when Kathleen Hiss, a kindly cousin, saved it from the garbage can. Mary C. left a quarter of a million dollars to Goucher, the women's college outside Baltimore, her alma mater, which somewhat upset John Hiss, another elderly cousin, who responded by throwing out most of her papers. She also left Al ten grand, and he remembers her kindly. Grandma's five pages deal almost exclusively with the family of her mother, who died when she was a year and a half old. "The Ancestry" — she wrote — "of Mary Lavinia Hiss on her Mother's side. Her family were English belonging to the Grundys who traced back to the Earl of Leicester, Lady Jane Grey belonging to the family tree." On page five of the notes she says that her father was Scotch-Irish.

Charlie and Minnie — as grandma was known — had five kids, and Charlie, who, according to his obituary, was "a man of genial disposition and had scores of friends," also looked after the six kids of an older brother, John Crowther Hiss, who had a heart attack and died in 1895 at the age of thirty-four. Minnie persuaded Charlie to find work for her only brother, Albert Hughes. The short, dapper Al Hughes became treasurer of Daniel Miller & Company and, depending on whom you speak to, either misinvested or made off with ten thousand bucks. Charlie paid off the debt by selling his own shares in the firm and leaving the company. Alger's Uncle Al stayed on as treasurer for the rest of his life. Charlie had been making forty to fifty grand a year, big money in those days, and was now broke. So he went down to North Carolina to see his oldest brother, George — the same George who later told my Uncle Bosley that the Hisses are Jewish — who was doing fine in the cotton business. George had been a black sheep — that is to say, as a youngster he was a sculptor and a drunk. Then he took the Keeley Cure (an early cold turkey sobering-up cure) and headed down to North Carolina and started making money. In later years he looked after the finances of almost all the Hisses in Baltimore. George offered Charlie half of a large cotton mill which he was about to purchase and urged him to move the family down to Charlotte. Charlie was ecstatic, and went back to Maryland to break the good news. If Charlie had taken George up on this offer he would have become a millionaire, but Minnie said: "Leave Baltimore? Leave my horse and carriage? Never! Surely you can see that the simple life they lead down there would never suit your wife and children."

On the first Saturday in April 1907 Charlie took his five kids for a long drive through Druid Hill Park. Sunday morning he called downstairs to Minnie and told her to summon the family physician. Then he cut his throat with a razor — "almost from ear to ear," the Baltimore *Sun* reported in its obit. "The razor was still grasped firmly in his hand." The headline on the obit was "CUT THROAT WITH RAZOR," but Al and his baby brother, Donald, were never told the truth about their dad's death and didn't find out until they overheard an old lady on the block gossiping about it. The *Sun* also said that Charlie had been "a prominent clubman, a member of the Baltimore Athletic Club, the Pimlico Country Club, Mystic Circle Lodge of Masons, and of the Merchants and Manufacturers Association." Minnie never remarried, and she never left Baltimore.

So Charlie was dead. Minnie had to give up her horse and carriage but she was still pretty well fixed — she had Charlie's paid-up $100,000 life insurance policy. And she had a house. And there was Uncle George. So for the next twenty-two years she was able to count on an income of five to six thousand dollars a year. "We were modest," as Al says, "but not, as Murray Kempton wrote, shabby genteel. There was plenty of gentility, but it wasn't particularly shabby." Minnie's money was looked after by a man at the Baltimore Fidelity Trust Company, who put it in the safest local blue chips, so she did fine until the Depression, when it turned out that stocks like Baltimore Gas and Electric and the B&O Railroad had been watered by speculators in the twenties.

Minnie was also left with five kids: Anna, thirteen; Mary, eleven; Bosley, almost seven; and the itty-bitties — as Cousin

Elizabeth Hiss Hartman, Mary's age, and still alive and in good shape, remembers them — Al, almost two and a half; and Donie, just three months. Aunt Lila, Charlie's sister, decided to move in immediately and help out. This left Aunt Lucy, another sister, living with and helping look after the six John Hiss children, the ones Charlie had helped look after, and looking in on Charlie's children whenever she could. Lila and Lucy were spinsters, or "unclaimed blessings," as they put it, who had both wanted to become schoolteachers but never did because their mother had told them it wasn't dignified. Al's only memory of Charlie is of trouser legs. "I have no recollection of the man above the knees." His first clear recollection is of Lila reading aloud from Bulfinch's *Fables*. Al thought Lila was wonderful: "a bouncy little person who read aloud by the hour from the Bible or King Arthur stories with the Arthur Rackham illustrations." And he liked Lucy too: "tremendously sympathetic and understanding. They were like the two sisters in the biblical tale. Lucy was Mary and Lila was Martha, who did all the work." Al once took a Sunday school prize for biblical studies. Lucy was the kind of woman who could persuade Cousin Elizabeth's mother to let Elizabeth go to China in 1930 to teach Chinese factory girls how to read and write — Elizabeth was thirty-six at the time. Lucy also wasn't quite sure at first about Al in 1948 when the shit hit the fan. She and Cousin Mary C. both wondered: How could anyone make up those charges if they weren't true? "Their faith was in Alger," Cousin Elizabeth explains it, "but it wasn't to the point where he had to be listened to."

It was a wonder Al didn't turn out gay. "My childhood was certainly female dominated," as he puts it. He became a prig instead. When Al was nineteen, big brother Bosley wrote him a letter addressed to "My dear worshipper of Virginity." Bosley, by then twenty-three, was what Al then called "a man about town," meaning he fucked girls. Al got engaged to a pretty blonde from New Orleans when he was in college, but they didn't fool around, and the first naked woman he saw was a not-very-happy-looking Indian whore in Tijuana when he was twenty-three himself and driving across the country with some buddies from Harvard Law School. He couldn't get it up on that occasion. Later in the trip they all checked into the cheapest hotel in Portland, Oregon, which turned out to be a whorehouse, and Al went upstairs with "a great big blousy blonde," who said: "Hurry up. Oh — what a mess." Back in Boston one night, a pal said, "Let's go find some girls," but neither of them knew where to look, so a taxi driver took them to a pretty black hooker. Al thought she was cute, but he couldn't do anything. He got into some pretty heavy petting with the daughter of his Cambridge boarding-house landlady. The girl kept asking Al to go to bed with her, but when she told him she was a virgin herself, Al said he wasn't going to deflower her because he wasn't going to marry her. He was still a virgin on his wedding night in 1929, when he was twenty-five.

There's a new women's phys. ed. building at the University of Texas named after Al's sister Anna. Miss Anna, as they called her down in Texas, was an unclaimed blessing who was good at sports and once scored fifty-six points in a girl's basketball game at the Sergeant School of Physical Education in Cambridge, Massachusetts, setting an all-time record. She was director of Physical Education at the U. of T. for almost fifty years, spent vast sums of collegiate money on new facilities, knew Ima Hogg, knew Lyndon and all the big Texas pols, taught Lady Bird, was beloved in Austin, and was always terrified of her job. She had all that money to spend because the Texas legislature before the turn of the century had irrevocably deeded vast tracts of useless wasteland to the university. When oil was inevitably discovered on the property, the best the legislature could do was pass a law stipulating that none of the oil revenues could be spent on salaries and must all go for construction, thus insuring that some dough got back to the local contractors. Al doesn't think Anna was a lesbian.

Mary, Al's other sister, was also good at sports. She was also very pretty, had lots of boyfriends, was bossy, and imitated her mother. She palled around with Cousin Elizabeth but snooted her because she went to a private school and Elizabeth didn't. Minnie pushed Mary to marry money and helped her get hitched to Elliot Emerson, a rich, charming, well-connected Boston stockbroker with a big car and a good line of gab who bought stocks on margin and went blooey in the smash. Al liked him, too, and found him quite captivating. Mary liked him better when he'd had money and so she ate some lye and committed suicide in 1929. Minnie and Elliot remained close friends.

Two men who meant anything to Al when he was small were his brother Bosley, four and a half years his senior, whom he adored, and the Reverend Mr. Wevill, rector of the local Reformed Episcopal church, a kindly bachelor whom Al kept up with over the years. He came to Al's first trial every day from his retirement in New Jersey — the FBI told the prosecution about this, suggesting it was an act to impress the jury — and Al later wrote him regular letters from the clink. Bos was a wild boy who had run away from home twice. He was very popular, very dashing, a good left-handed tennis player, and good-looking, although he had pretty big ears, like all the Hisses. He grew up to be six-one, an inch taller than Al, quite tall for those days. He was, as Al remembers him, witty, frivolous, sophisticated, skeptical, and all but cynical. Bos wanted to be a writer and spent a winter on the Eastern Shore of Maryland, where the family summered,

collecting notes about local characters, but the only job he
ever got was police court reporter for the Baltimore *Sun*,
where he persuaded the management to give columnist Clay-
ton Fritchey a start. Bos was a young snob who liked being a
police court reporter who went to fancy parties at night. He
had girlfriends Al remembers as Scott Fitzgerald girls — Bos
bedded down with them, remember — and he was always able
to twist all the women in the family around his little finger.
He drank a lot, which probably had something to do with his
fears of what the women wanted to do with *his* little finger, and
contracted Bright's disease, an alcohol-induced kidney ailment
where you can't pee. Al thinks Bos could have gotten over it
if he hadn't been nursed by Minnie, whose favorite he was.
Instead, he went back to the *Sun*, started drinking again, got
sick again, had an affair with Margaret Owen, an older
woman, a very successful interior decorator in New York
whom Al never liked — he considered her "underbred." In
the summer of 1926, the summer before Al went off to law
school, Bos was dying. He married Margaret, who rented a
house in Harrison, New York, in Westchester County, and she,
Bos, and Al spent the summer there. Al had the job of driving
Bos to the hospital, where the doctors punctured his abdomen
to drain the water off. Bosley died that November.

Baby Donie, the other itty-bitty, who shared with Al the
back bedroom at the top of Minnie's house on Linden Avenue, has just moved permanently to a big house called Sherwood Forest on the Eastern Shore about a mile and a half
from the house the Hisses spent the summers in seventy years
ago. Before Covington, Donie did almost exactly what Al did:
Johns Hopkins, Alpha Delta Phi, Harvard, legal secretary to
Oliver Wendell Holmes, government service in the New
Deal. Whit Chambers even said Al and Donie had been
members of the same Red Commie pinko spy cell, but Donie

never got hauled up on charges like Al and went to Covington instead of the pen. He's a friendly man, has those big ears, and he and Al get on fine. Donie has a tidewater southern accent; Al doesn't. They both have soft voices. Donie's eyes have gone bad; Al's inner ears aren't what they used to be.

When they were both small, Al used to tell Donie there were bears under his bed, and Donie would howl, and Minnie would climb all the way to the top of the house, which she hated, to see what was the matter, but Donie would never peach on Al. He has still never forgiven Al for this. In church Minnie always sat between them to keep them quiet, and Al would give Donie the giggles by pretending to steal a hatpin from Minnie when she wasn't looking and then pretend to stick it into the fat rumps of the ladies in the pew in front. Minnie could never figure out how Al was causing trouble because he could sit still and look good. Donie was a good athlete.

Al was a runt and didn't achieve his growth until the year after he graduated from public high school in Baltimore and Minnie sent him off to a prep school in Massachusetts for a year. It was the first year he spent away from home. Cousin Elizabeth remembers Al as a quiet, happy child and also as always the brightest of the five kids in his family and the six kids in her family. Al remembers that he never got any attention from Minnie. Anna got attention because she was the oldest, Mary because she was the prettiest, Bos because he was the first son, Donie because he was the baby. What Minnie said to Al was: "Well, Alger, you'll never be a pretty boy, but at least you have good posture." He suddenly got lots of attention from Minnie after he was indicted, but it was all tease and sympathy. You poor boy, mother won't leave you now. This helped smarten Al up vis-à-vis Minnie, and he ducked into the briar patch and started getting happy. In the end it turned out that Al was the one who most thoroughly got away from Min. Donie's doing all right, but of course he hasn't had Al's advantages. Anna never got near a man, and Bos and Mary didn't last long.

2. The Runt

AL IS SIX FEET TALL, half an inch taller than I am, although he has a slight stoop these days, and walks carefully, watching his balance. But until he was sixteen he was a runt who weighed less than a hundred and fifteen pounds, so small that he won a lot of track medals in high school because the coach could put him up against younger kids. The runt lived at 1427 Linden Avenue, a tiny detached three-story house in a middle-class neighborhood of row houses put up in the 1880s, whose boundaries were an armory several blocks to the south and Al's public school — No. 14 — four or five blocks to the north. The house had a bathroom, gas lights, and was heated by coal fires in Franklin stoves. Al and Donie got to haul the coal up to the different rooms from the cellar.

There certainly were a lot of women in sight. In addition to Minnie, Lila, and Lucy, there was Fräulein Hogendorf, from whom he took German lessons on Saturday mornings; the lady across the street, from whom he took piano lessons — she lived in the first apartment house in the neighborhood (Donie and Bosley were given violin lessons); the Saturday art classes of Marjorie Martinet — easel painting, charcoal pencil sketches of still lifes, busts, occasionally models, sometimes trees and houses on a trip to the country; there was a dancing school teacher — the runt had to put on a blue serge suit and knickers and white cotton gloves and he found the lessons very dull because he wasn't allowed to dance very often with the most popular girls; there were all the old lady teachers at P.S. 14 for whom he fussed over his assignments and homework; Grandmother Hughes, Minnie's stepmother, who lived nearby; lots of girlfriends of his two big sisters, Mary and Anna; Tege Wrightson, a sort of cousin and best friend of Minnie's who lived on a big farm on the Eastern Shore of Maryland where the family spent the summers with Tege's family; and Cory Roberts, Tege's big tough friendly sensible black cook. Most of the kids in Miss Martinet's art class were girls. The only men in Al's vicinity were Mr. Mann, a patent attorney who went to Minnie's church and at her invitation frequently came over to Sunday dinner or took the Hiss kids to his house "to provide a man's influence"; the Reverend Mr. Wevill, who took the boys' Bible group hiking on Saturdays; and Bosley, who as Cory used to say, "Must have got the man on him very early." Al still has the Bible signed by Mr. Wevill, presented for excellence in Biblical Studies. After Al got out of jail, he went to see him out near Newark. He remembers Mr. Wevill as "very dapper and sweet." Mr. Mann, on the other hand, "didn't do many things boys were interested in. I don't remember any hikes with him. But he was useful at World Series time. His office was directly across from the *Sun* building's big electric scoreboard reconstruction of the games."

The center of family life was the dinner table, a big table in a small dining room always crowded with Mary's friends or Bosley's. Al's cousin Elizabeth, who came over occasionally, remembers how Minnie required all the children to answer questions about national and local history. Other guests were family — cousins and Grandma Hughes. The kids loved Cousin Annie Johnson, because she always forgot she had lumbago in her back and always stood up from the table and said, "Well, Minnie . . . оооh!" Grandma Hughes put down the wife of an engineer cousin from Chicago who said her husband was a wonderful engineer because when he tied his shoes the two bows were always exactly the same size. Grandma Hughes said she didn't know about engineers but she'd always heard they were people who could make the two halves of the Pennsylvania Railroad Tunnel meet in the middle, not just people who could do up their boots. But Grandma Hughes was terrified of Minnie. Grandma Hughes used to love to break up her toast and put it in her soup, but she always glanced surreptitiously at her stepdaughter before she did this because if Minnie caught her at it, she would say, "Maw — don't do that!"

Minnie's rule was "keep the conversation general. Talk about 'topics.'" When Bosley would criticize someone, or when Alger, copying Bosley, would, her response was "that's like your grandmother's itching powder — mean fun." Her instructions were "Don't criticize. You can always find some good in everybody." So she would introduce her two daughters like this: "Mary is my pretty daughter, and Anna is my active daughter." "Donald," she said once, "you have very good color. In your ears." The rule was always say something nice, and in Minnie's favorite hypothetical example, if a lady asks you if you like her hat and you don't, you tell her she has nice shoes. As Al once said to Donie — "You must remember. She's never lost an argument."

"Mortified" was one of Minnie's favorite words. When she was upset or displeased she always said she was "mortified." Little Al kept a notebook of words he didn't know. When a preacher in church would use a word he hadn't heard, it went into the book. He says, "I learned how to be careful in speaking from the boredom of sermons."

I guess the time Minnie was most "mortified" by the runt was the day she led a delegation of women to the mayor's office to complain about the quality of education in the city. Al was then sixteen, a senior at City College, a big downtown high school he didn't like, where the teachers were mostly men. Before Minnie could get her education pitch launched the mayor asked her, "Mrs. Hiss, do you know where the truant officer found your son this morning?"

"No," she said, stopped cold.

"In a poolroom."

Al hooked school at least thirty days in high school. He saw a lot of nickel movies — Theda Bara — and learned how to shoot a pretty good game of pool, although he had trouble reaching over the table. He also smoked cigarettes. His marks in high school were only so-so — he graduated with a seventy-nine-plus average, but only because after Minnie's mortification he was told he wouldn't graduate unless he buckled down, so he crammed for the last three months. Track was the one thing he liked in high school — running and lying on the infield grass. These days Al bums cigarettes occasionally but won't buy 'em. He has a good collection of pipes and smokes a special mixture of burley, latakia, and perique invented by an old man he got to know after he got out of jail — Tom Cleland, the artist and typographer who designed the famous wheel of fortune for the first cover of *Fortune*. Al also likes Cuban cigars when he can get them. He's been known to slip a couple in his raincoat on the way home from Europe. Donie hooked school only once.

Minnie was around the house less than most of the family, since her time was taken up with many women's clubs. There was the Mothers Club, the Women's Club, and the Arundel

Club, where the ladies heard lectures on civic affairs and played bridge. She occasionally punished the boys, but both Donie and Alger learned how to escape. When she smacked their hands with a hairbrush, they would jerk them away and then pretend it hurt more than it did, and she would stop. Alger remembers bending over for a couple of spankings, but he says when you got spanked all you had to do was jump and yell. What he got punished mostly for was teasing Donie. Alger had a temper and would beat on Donie — until Donie, who wasn't a runt, got to be as big as Alger. Donie says he only retaliated against Alger once. Alger was standing outside the front door and told Donie that unless he let him in he would break every bone in Donie's body. Donie picked up a tennis racket, and when he let Alger in he hit him with it.

As a boy, Alger didn't like Mary too much — he thought she was stuck up. He worshiped Bosley and tried to be just like him, but he was also jealous of Bos and didn't show him much affection. Donie worshiped both his brothers but was scared of Alger.

Alger liked to feel he had himself under control and he considered emotional displays undignified. The family had a fat old brindle bulldog named Jill, who could fart noiselessly, and Alger liked to speculate how everyone except him would cry if anything happened to the dog. When the dog was hit by a a car, he bawled, and learned, he said, "that the theoretical control of emotion was not the same thing as the actual control of emotion."

Alger was a businessman. Cousin Elizabeth remembers that he had a "most normal bringing-up. He was never unhappy. He cooperated with his dominating mother." Alger remembers that he "spent an awful lot of his life in the streets, backyards, and parks rollerskating and playing baseball and football." Huntington Cairns, the author, connoisseur, and former secretary of the National Gallery, who was tackle on the neighborhood football team, remembers that Alger had no time for games because he was so busy with his water business. And the son of Mr. Beatson, Minnie's banker, loathed Alger because his mother kept telling him what a good boy Alger was. The water business, one of Alger's two businesses, was a big operation. A lot of people in the Linden Avenue neighborhood distrusted tap water in those days and were willing to pay a nickel a quart for water from a spring in Druid Hill Park. So Alger and his friend Fritz Geyer, a German kid — the Hisses stopped seeing the Geyers in 1916 when a German U-boat paid a ceremonial call on Baltimore and the Geyers, like other German families, entertained the officers — hauled a long wagon with a big demijohn and a lot of small quart bottles up the hill near the park to the spring, where at least a dozen other wagons were loading up with water. Al took home two dollars a week from this business. "My favorite memory," he says, "is a little shack at the edge of the park that sold the most delicious fried oyster sandwiches for a nickel. You couldn't pass up those sandwiches even though they each cost a quart of spring water. But I was paying for them with money I'd made myself. God, they were good!"

Al's other business was selling squabs to neighbors. Bosley had started keeping pigeons on the roof in back of the house over the maid's room and later took on Alger and Donie as partners and made them do the work. They built a bigger coop in the backyard and kept at least forty birds. They sold some of the birds live to other pigeon fanciers, and some of these birds would fly back to 1427 Linden Avenue after being sold, so the boys sold them over and over again. Donie refused to kill the birds for the squab trade, so Alger either chopped off their heads or wrung their necks. The business was called the BAD Hiss Boys — for Bosley, Alger, Donald — and it flourished until rats got to the birds. At this point D wanted out — the feed bills were using up his entire fifty cents weekly allowance, and he wasn't getting any return. B and A told him he couldn't get out unless all three partners agreed, but Minnie interrupted and offered to take over Donie's interest, at which point the business collapsed.

The place in the world all the Hiss kids loved best was Sherwood Manor, Aunt Tege Wrightson's four-hundred-acre farm on the Miles River on the Eastern Shore of Maryland. The kids would lie out on the grass under the trees with the two Wrightson boys, Bill and Hastings, and dream about how when they were all grown up they would all get a place together down there and farm it. "It was paradisiacal," Al says. Minnie's best friend, Tege, was Grandma Hughes's niece. Tege thought of herself as a lady but was a pretty decent person. She crooked her little finger when drinking a cup of tea. She came from Virginia and liked to tell stories about how her father went out for rides with Robert E. Lee. Her husband, Uncle Josh Wrightson, she said was a Chesterfield. Charlie Hiss, before his death, had checked out Uncle Josh and reported that he was an ex-drunk who had abandoned the sauce, so Tege married him.

Baltimore, in the first years of this century, was turning into a big industrial city, but on Linden Avenue it still seemed like a sleepy southern town with a good university — Johns Hopkins. Professors came to dinner parties in Baltimore. The Eastern Shore was the old, old rural South. It still is. In St. Michaels, the "town that fooled the British" and the town closest to Tege's farm, they still talk about how, in 1812, they put out all the lights one night, except for a couple in the steeple. So the English fleet, which was anchored offshore, thought they were further inland than they were and fired over their heads doing no damage at all, except for one cannonball that fell down a chimney and broke the leg of an old lady who was knitting by the fire. The big social event of the year in St. Michaels, as it always has been, is the annual Chesapeake Bay log canoe race.

The Wrightson House — it's still there — had the Miles River, a Chesapeake Bay estuary, to one side, and a couple of creeks to the front and back. The farm raised wheat, corn, and tomatoes as cash crops, all its own food, and cows, sheep, chickens, turkeys, pigs, and guinea hens. Cap'n Ned Dawson, a black-sheep Wrightson cousin, lived in a room at the top of the house and in the old days had had a grain boat in which he took the farm's wheat up to Baltimore for sale. He was the overseer of the farm and ran its machinery, and the plates on which he ate were always boiled. Minnie said it was because he had syphilis, and Tege said she could never leave him alone in the house with the maid. The black farm hands were old-timers — one of the Wrightson boys said that the family always gave Tege the old men when they were finished with them on their own farms. Uncle Jake, one of Tege's hands, was an ex-slave who couldn't read or tell time. He used to pee in his pants, and when Tege would tell him to change his clothes he would tell her: "Yo' smell yo'self, Missy — put that where you chews!" He liked to drink from the pump in the yard, and when Cory, the cook, told him not to, he would tell her: "The Lamb drink out of the spiggot spout hole — why can't I?" Cory stories and Uncle Jake stories were just about the only stories about his childhood that Al ever told me when I was growing up, and he and Donie, who still swap 'em when they get together, tell these tales and tales about Justice Holmes with a lot of pleasure, and they enjoy imitating the voices of the characters and telling the stories the way they heard them.

Al's got good stories about the rest of his life, like the story about Anthony Eden pissing at Yalta in the men's room and getting so nervous when he realized Joe Stalin was standing in line behind him that he started spraying the walls — but Al sometimes needs prompting to tell stories like that, and I think I only heard that one for the first time a couple of years ago. I can remember only three Minnie stories from my childhood: one about how Al, who all his life has loved going to the theater, and who at the time of the story had saved up his pennies to see a play called *The Bad Man*, tipped over backward at the dinner table one day and smashed the curved glass panels on the front of a curio cabinet. So Minnie told him, "No 'Bad Man' for you, young man." The other stories were about habits of Minnie's — she would occasionally serve pistachio ice cream, which was expensive and her favorite flavor, as a special treat for Al, who hated it. Also, when she wanted you to do something at dinnertime, she would wait until you were just sinking into your chair and then say, "While you're up . . ."

Uncle Jake used to complain to Cory that she had wised up one of the Wrightson boys — "That Hastings has been ruined! I'd say, 'Gimme some of your Christmas' " — meaning candy — " 'and he used to come a-runnin'. Now he comes a-fightin'." In the winter Cory liked to sit in the kitchen in the evening and hated to go up to her cold bedroom, and would get Uncle Jake to keep her company by telling him it was only eight, eight-thirty, nine o'clock. "Hm! Hm!" he would say. "That all? Seemed later to me."

"Cory was the bulwark of Sherwood Manor," says Donie. "She kept us level-headed, got us to do things, and introduced an element of reality into our matriarchy. She brought us all up, really took an interest in us, saw through Tege's pretentiousness, and hated Uncle Josh, who was not an ex-drunk. She had a window in her kitchen which looked out to the barn, so she could see him go down there before breakfast to get his jug."

Minnie and Cory were the only two people on the farm who would stand up to Uncle Josh. Cory wouldn't let Josh kill

Alger or the older Wrightson boy the time they found the jug and poured it out, and Cory would tell Tege whenever she defended her husband, "Yes — he's a Chesterfield — burned all the way down to the butt." Cory lived in a little black village near the farm. She'd worked in a boarding house before she went to work for Tege. One of the boarders was a fussy woman who told Cory every morning that the coffee wasn't hot enough. So Cory baked a cup in the oven, cooled off the handle at the pump, filled the cup with coffee, and served it. The woman's lip stuck to the cup and coffee flew across the table. There were no more complaints.

When Al was a boy, Eastern Shore farms like Tege's operated just about the same way they had before Emancipation. Neighbors were just beginning to move out West because the soil was getting depleted, but nobody paid much attention until World War I when the big new farms in the Middle West with their modern equipment suddenly started badly underselling the Eastern Shore farmers. The farms that turn a profit on the Eastern Shore today are twelve- to fifteen-hundred acres, completely mechanized outfits. When Josh died after the First World War, Tege's farm was heavily mortgaged, and she finally sold it in '34 and moved to St. Michaels. The Hiss boys spent every summer at Tege's working in the fields and the vegetable garden, crabbing, fishing, sailing, swimming — until they were twelve or thirteen and went off to camps in New England. Since there were two Wrightson boys and three Hiss boys there were just enough boys for a scrub baseball game, except when Alger, who wanted to read as many books as Bos had, sometimes went off into the house or under a tree with a book. Then Bosley would yell, "Bookworm!" and jump on him.

The first time Al ever went anywhere out of Baltimore by himself was when he was twelve and took the train up to Camp Wildwood in Maine. It was a memorable trip because when Al sat down in the smoker the man he was sitting next to was Chick Fewster, second baseman for the New York Yankees. Al was already a second baseman because of Chick Fewster. Baltimore was baseball mad in those days — the old Baltimore Orioles were an International League team who sent men like Ruth to the majors, and Al was a stat freak who knew everyone's average, and Chick Fewster had been his hero since the day Al had gone to visit Bos in the hospital after Bos had his appendix out. This was when Al was nine. It was the same day that Chick Fewster got beaned in Baltimore, and Al saw Chick get wheeled into the operating theater and heard the doctors say they were going to cut out a piece of his skull and no one knew if he was going to live or die. Chick lived and went back to baseball, and when Al mustered up the courage to talk to him on the train, it turned out Chick was a nice guy who would talk to a kid. He let Al feel the soft place in his head, told Al he could write to him and even wrote back. He once later even offered Al World Series tickets in New York, but Al couldn't talk Minnie into letting him go.

Donie was sent to a different camp, Pemigewasett, in New Hampshire, where he had a counselor named Whoppo Griswold — who was considered a bully. Whoppo was later known as Erwin Griswold, dean of Harvard Law School and solicitor general of the U.S., a man Al came to admire. When the boys went off to camp, so did Minnie. She worked one summer as assistant to Mrs. Gulick, a lady who ran Camp Lanakila and the Aloha Camps, where Anna and Mary went, in Vermont. When the family was far-flung, Minnie put instructions for everyone else in letters to her sisters-in-law and looked for constant report letters in reply from every outpost. A "Dear Lila and Lucy, Love from Minnie" letter written July 4, 1921, which concludes with a P.S. perpendicular to the rest of the letter ("P.S. Gen. Pershing's son, Warren, is in the tent with Donald. Minnie") begins:

"Now while all the campers are asleep, being quiet hour, is a fine opportunity to send you a few lines. I have found no time for writing except a few letters to Bosley, the two boys and Mary. As I found Mary had been in bed ever since Maude's wedding [a Smith classmate of Mary's] and was feeling very uncomfortable, I tried to attend to a number of little things she had been unable to do and did some shopping for her. The doctor hopes she may feel better by the middle of this month. Having had trouble in the early winter, she will have to be very careful to prevent anything of that kind again.

"Bosley and Edward Norris are in New York at 210 Madison Ave. I know he would love to get a letter from you. I hope to hear from him again tomorrow. Alger and Donald were very busy and happy at Camp Red Cloud, Brackney P.O., Pa. when I last heard from them. I also hope for another letter from them tomorrow.

"I started taking one of the crafts, and am making a silver pendant and hope to work in pottery, basket weaving, and weaving either a rug or a scarf. Then we have such an excellent trained nurse, who has classes in home nursing and I am taking that course. We have a very remarkable naturalist, Mr. Kinsey, and his wife who take out parties to learn to know the birds, others to know wild flowers, other trips for pathfinding, camp cookery, how to know the stars, and how to find your way through the woods on a dark night, and how to make a fire out of doors, even if it is raining. I went with the party that left at 5:15 this morning and learned to know about twelve birds. So you see there is no danger of getting lazy up here. Violet, the cook, is such a marvelous cook, and our little dietician plans such well balanced meals, that it is only the steep climb up these hills that will keep me from gaining. We get up at 6 A.M., at 6:15 are over at the bungalow, where Anna puts us through a vigorous setting up drill.

"Now do write and let me know all about your plans. I

must add Anna is certainly a valuable addition to camp, everyone says. She is so full of pep and ideas and never seems to exhaust her supply. Love to both of you and Nina if she is with you. Let her share this letter with you. I will write her sometime soon."

Minnie four years later from Lanakila, again to Dear Lila and Lucy, the summer before Alger's senior year in college: "A letter from Alger this morning informed me that Anna had developed a very good figure, and was better looking than he had ever seen her. I am surprised that Bosley has taken all this time on the trip home. [Bosley had his kidney disease by this time.] The doctor could hardly have objected if he had known he would take it as slowly as he has. Poor Alger is certainly going through a hardening process. He says the coolest place has been 112° and they drill for hours in the sun. If he stands this he is certainly ready for almost any kind of endurance test. He seems to be standing it. [Al was cadet colonel in the Johns Hopkins ROTC — he was later a second looie in the Army reserves for a number of years — commission never activated.] I am glad he can go down to Sherwood Manor for the weekends.

"Mr. Gulick came over in the morning and gave the boys a very interesting talk on evolution. Of course he did not call it that but his illustration was the pyramids of Egypt and in a very simple way he explained that the first strata of the pyramid was inanimate matter, so called. Then he explained how alive that matter was and gave the boys the scientific explanation of ions. On this first strata, vegetable matter drew its life from it and formed the second. Then on to the next which was animal life, next human life developed, next the superior men, experts, rulers, presidents, etc., and the top of the structure was the most superior, Jesus Christ. Four of our fine men counselors gave us a quartet after the sermon and of course we all sang a number of lovely hymns. It is indeed a wonderfully fine life that these boys live here. I love the life here, it is physically invigorating, mentally stimulating, and spiritually also. I hope that Anna and Mrs. Shepherd will be up here for August.

"Write to me. I shall be eager to hear of your plans. I must write to Bosley and Alger, so no more tonight, but lots of love, Devotedly, Minnie."

In other letters from Minnie the following items turn up:

"You know my fondness for the dining car, well I am living up to my past record and had three delicious meals there yesterday, one the evening before, and plan on three today. If you have the March number of The Atlantic read on page 379 Dr. Eliot's article on the Great Religious Revival . . . Urge the boys to take dinner with you on Sunday, even if Alger has to leave early and get his lessons. If you or Lillian have the Last Days of Pompeii, I wish you would give it to Donald to read. Alger could get his dinner at the fraternity house, and he prefers to be in his own room where he has all his own papers and books."

This may seem repetitive, but remember, in the Hiss household the cards and letters never stopped coming. They never stopped getting saved either, which is how I have some today. A final Minnieature is taken from a letter from Florida, written in February '26, the last winter of Bosley's life: "Bosley has at last consented to let me read aloud to him. He has never cared to be read to, or to read aloud himself. I think he finds it a relief now to not use his eyes so much.

"It is a great source of comfort to know you are keeping an oversight of Donald and Alger. I do hope Alger does not have grippe. I urge him in every letter I send to keep up the tonic he is taking and take raw eggs and milk. He is using up so much vitality that he must keep himself in good condition."

Alger was twenty-one at that point, a senior at Hopkins. Bosley, before he got Bright's disease, had walked out on

Minnie a few years previously, when she said she'd clean up his room if he'd read the editorials in the Baltimore *Sun* out loud to her. Al, who loved reading out loud — he and mom read all of *Moby Dick* to each other the first year they were married — was still mixing raw eggs and milk together when I was a kid, and he got me into the habit. I guess it was the only thing I ever saw him do in the kitchen except wash the dishes or get ice out of the icebox, although these days he can find himself around the place O.K. when Isabel isn't there to cook for him or he isn't eating out at a burger joint he likes around the corner where the Greek countermen call him "Professor." Al used to add a little vanilla extract and a couple of spoonfuls of sugar to his egg and milk, and then stirred everything up in a glass with a fork. As far as I know, that's Alger Hiss's only recipe, except for his Fishhouse Punch recipe — dark rum, light rum, brandy, peach brandy, and iced tea. I like making punches myself and can recommend Al's concoction, except that if you replace the iced tea with vodka, tequila, and Calvados parties don't take so long to warm up. Al's milkshake isn't too bad, but the egg whites never fully dissolve. When Al was a kid he read aloud to his brothers and sisters. Aunt Lila not only read stories and the Bible out loud to the kids, but she and Minnie and Aunt Lucy read prayers from the *Book of Common Prayer* to the whole family before church on Sundays. The children were not allowed to read the funny papers in the Baltimore *Sun* on Sundays, so Donie and Al always got up before everyone else and sneaked downstairs and read them on the stoop. Not out loud.

Of the surviving family letters only one deals with anything other than official business — instructions and reports of activities and illness. In 1925 Lucy took off for a quick visit to Uncle George in Charlotte. Lila, who was sixty at the time, was miffed. "In vain," she wrote her fifty-eight-year-old sister, "have we looked for some word telling of your safe arrival at Bertha and George's home. While you know, I am not of the disposition to worry over imaginary evils, I can but wonder why you or Bertha could not have written on the sheet of paper which I enclosed in the self addressed and stamped envelope. 'Arrived safe met by Bertha.' (or whomsoever) 'Will write later.' sealed and dropped in the box at the station, certainly would have been received this morning — The third mail having been delivered today — Nina having some of Job's or his wife's temperament thinks it very strange you did not go to the phone and send a telegram to state your 'safe arrival and no one ill' at 302.

"I trust you had a comfortable journey and all went well."

The middle of the letter talks about two nieces who didn't visit "because each had imperative work at home" and says "was surprised to learn you were on the way to Charlotte — Of course I was invited also — but I had marketing to do and besides wanted to go to Lillian's for a while."

The last paragraph says "Bosley is out again. Dr. [illegible] did not pronounce his trouble *Bright's*, finally — so 'Richard is himself again.' I know you will not feel like writing much or often — but why did Bertha write to you to come so suddenly? Love for each one from yours lovingly, Lila."

Lucy kept this letter, like all the others, the rest of her life, and then it went to family historian Cousin Mary C., whom she spent her last years with, and Mary C. never threw anything out, so this letter with a two-cent stamp is still around. The letters and some photographs are about the only family artifacts that survive, except for some silver knives and forks of Anna's. When I turned twenty-one Al gave me his dad's gold pocket watch and his gold cuff links and shirt studs. I saved the watch a couple of years later when I got robbed in Central Park with a long sentimental plea but lost it the next year. The cuff links disappeared at the laundry when I left them in a shirt, and the studs lasted until just the other day when my

apartment was ripped off. I've got some old clothes of Al's —
a top hat, believe it or not, and cutaway coat Al had made by
a Scottish tailor in Paris when he came into a small inheritance
his last year at law school that moths now chip their teeth on.
Burglars won't touch the thing. I haven't worn it since my
Episcopalian phase, but of course I've put on weight since my
Episcopalian phase. Nina, mentioned in Lila's letter, was
Lila's and Lucy's oldest sister, sixty-one at the time of the
letter. She married a Crowther, which is why Alger and
Bosley Crowther, former *New York Times* movie critic, are
cousins.

Lucy also hung on all her life to a desk journal for 1880, the
year she turned twenty-three. The book has a single entry
dated January 18 and titled "Barriers Burned Away," in beautiful copperplate handwriting. I don't know the name of the
man she was writing about.

"Disappointment in love is one of the severest tests of
character in man or woman. Some sink into weak senti-
mentality, and mope and languish; some become listless;
apathetic, and float down the current of existence like drift-
wood. Men are often harsh and cynical, and rail at the sex
to which their mothers and sisters belong. Sometimes a man
inflicts *a well nigh fatal wound and leaves his victim to cure
it as best she may*. From that time forth she may be like the
wronged Indian, who slays as many white men as she can.
Not a few on finding they cannot enter the beautiful paradise
of happy love, plunge into imbruting vice, and drown not only
their disappointment, but themselves in dissipation. If women
have true metal in them (and they usually have) they become
unselfishly devoted to others, and by gentle, self-denying ways
seek to impart to others about them the happiness denied to
themselves.

"We take memory and character with us from land to land,
from youth to age, from this world to the other, from time

through eternity. Sad then is the lot of those who ever carry the elements of their own torture with them.

"God can console and make up every loss to his children, but the passionate human heart, with its intense human love, clings to its idol nonetheless.

"The Bible like a casket made of most precious stones and costly gems, banded together by golden links and casings, and the casket filled with treasures from many lands, each perfect of its kind — every stone traced with a truth and meaning of its own, which long years of patient study would hardly suffice to quite unfold, even to the diligent student; and yet, the stones, when held up to the light, whether by the hand of sage or child, always revealed something, always caught a glimmer from the far off sky, and with every change of position, a new radiance, just as we do with Bible words. 'Fear thou not, for I am with thee.' "

3. Mr. Hopkins Meets Pritsy Pru and the Great Dissenter

W HEN AL SCRAPED through high school, still small, he was only sixteen, and Minnie decided he was too young and too little for college. So she sent him off for a postgraduate stint to Powder Point Academy, a boys' prep school in Duxbury, Massachusetts, a couple of miles from Elliot and Mary's house. I guess I should say Mary Ann's house, because that is what she took to calling herself in the Boston area. It turned out that Al liked the school a lot. "It wasn't," he says, "that Minnie was impractical. She was just unloving." This was the first year that Al spent away from home and he grew so fast that by springtime when he managed, by a lot of sweat, to get on the school baseball team, he was already so gangly he had trouble fielding ground balls, they were so far away from his hands.

This transformation fits right in with Al's own theory about himself. He thinks he's a sedentary sort of guy who likes to make a nest wherever he is. He can be happy anywhere, but then someone always comes along and pushes him somewhere else, and it turns out he's even happier in the next place. He was happy with his first law firm job after Harvard, with one of the biggest, oldest corporation firms in Boston, and saw himself being a Boston lawyer the rest of his life.

But Al was married to mom by that point, and she hated Boston and wanted to get down to New York where the action was. So he joined a big corporation firm in New York and was all set to stay there indefinitely, when Professor Felix Frankfurter of the Harvard Law School, his favorite professor, told him it was his duty to go to Washington and join the New Deal. Then he had the time of his life in Washington and became a rising star about whom people whispered: "Possible secretary of state." After World War II he thought about going back to Boston, but then he got on a boat for London, for the first regular meeting of the United Nations General Assembly, and John Foster Dulles, who was on the same boat, offered him a foundation job as president of the Carnegie Endowment for International Peace. He loved this job and was all set to settle into being a foundation functionary for the rest of his days, when along came Whittaker Chambers and Dick Nixon and the Hiss case, and everything changed again. The Hiss case he thinks of these days as a "fortunate-unfortunate accident," one of an endless series of "fortunate-unfortunate accidents." Subsequent to the Hiss case he was a happy prisoner and then a happy printing salesman. Now he's a happy lawyer again. A couple of years after he got out of jail, he happened to run into one of the senior partners of his old Boston firm, who said, "You know, Alger, I sometimes wish you'd never left Choate, Hall and Stewart." "Me too," said Al.

The best thing at Powder Point Academy was George Pike, the sports coach, who straightened Al out, "taught me a couple of lessons," as Al says. Al was a second baseman because Chick Fewster was his idol, but also because he was a light hitter, a fast runner, and a good fielder, with an arm that wasn't strong enough to be accurate on the long throw from third. He was an "intellectual player," as he puts it, and thought out every move before the pitcher delivered. "If the ball goes here, I'll throw it there," etc. At the plate he held the bat almost straight up, near his shoulder, and it wasn't until he went to jail that he ever changed his batting stance. At Lewisburg, he started holding the bat back and his arms out and swinging away. The last time he ever hit a baseball in his life was in a scrub game in the prison yard when he was in his late forties, and "Pop," as they called him, surprised the hell out of all the young guys down there by hitting a home run clean between the left fielder and the center fielder that rolled all the way to the wall.

At Powder Point one day Alger told George Pike that he wasn't going to play against a visiting team because they had a nigger. George Pike just said, "Well, you don't have to play, there's the bench." Nobody else on the Powder Point team followed Al's example. "The Confederacy," he says, "didn't rise again." So he sat there and noticed that the team played just as well, if not better, without him and that everybody seemed to like the nigger. Pike never mentioned the incident afterward, and Al played in all the other games. What he liked was he'd been allowed to make his own decision. This was something new: "All we got from Minnie was preaching."

Lesson number 2 from George Pike came later in the season. Al was playing second. There was a man on third, one out. The next batter hit a soft pop just over the Powder Point pitcher's head, and he couldn't handle it. Al charged in. "I went ass over tincups, couldn't come up with the ball, and the run scored. But I thought to myself, 'I gave it one hell of a try.' In the dressing room after the game, Pike said about the play — and not particularly to me, 'Clumsy fool.'"

Al spent two terms at Powder Point, fall and spring. Elliot, who still had money in those days — this was why Mary was now calling herself Mary Ann — let Al drive his Cadillac roadster, and Al drove it into a tree, but he did more damage to the tree than he did to the car. The winter term Al lived at home and went to the Maryland Institute of Art and studied drawing and printmaking. He says he soon decided he had no talent for art and that his real interest in the place was a girl in his class who had two other boyfriends. She necked with Al on the staircases, but didn't want to be seen with him when one of the boyfriends, a tough guy, came around. The other boyfriend was a jock from Donie's old school, Friends School, and she could handle this guy too. One day he was carrying her around piggyback and when he wouldn't put her down, she peed all over his letter sweater.

The next fall Minnie decided Al was ready for college, and he entered the class of 1926 at Johns Hopkins University, which means, of course, he celebrated his fiftieth reunion last year. "I had a ball in college," he says, a fact amply attested to by the 1926 *Hullabaloo*, the college yearbook, which shows that Al was president of the student council his senior year; a Romance languages and history major — he was thinking of entering the foreign service; Phi Beta Kappa; a member of Alpha Delta Phi, the fanciest fraternity on campus (this was thanks to Bos, who'd been an Alpha Delt a few years before); vice president of Omicron Delta Kappa, "one of the highest honors attainable . . . only 3% of the undergraduate enrollment is eligible for election . . ."; lieutenant colonel of the campus ROTC unit and a member of Scabbard and Blade, the honorary military society founded in 1905 at the University of Wisconsin; a member of Pi Delta Epsilon, the national honorary journalistic fraternity and publishers of *The Blue Blackmail*, "a Thoroughgoing Exposé of Corrupt and Imaginarily Corrupt Campus Conditions"; a member of the Cane Club, "a few genial souls who believe in the old old ideals of chivalry, courtesy and honor . . . the white carnation symbolizing purity, the canc clegance, the stately carriage drawn by prancing steeds courtliness"; a member of the Cotillion Club, which ran the campus cotillions and Saturday Tea Dances; and secretary-treasurer of the Tudor and Stuart Club — "the Club's library includes one of the most valuable Spenser collections in the country." And that's only half of it, because he was also president of the Barnstormers, the campus actors, portraying the title role in *His Majesty Bunker Bean*. And he was editor-in-chief of the *News-Letter*. I think we can skip the rest of it.

Al liked all his courses and got top marks but suspected that the courses were all guts, and one reason he went on to Harvard Law School, which had a reputation for being tough, was to test his brain and see if the brain could take it (the brain stood up fine). Among the three teachers he liked best at Hopkins were his Greek teacher, Carol Wight, honorary president of the class of '26, a stockbroker who had been wiped out in the panic of '07, had then had a nervous breakdown and left his wife and child to go to sea. In the fo'c's'le he read Greek, so when he went home again he became a Greek teacher.

Spanish teacher José Robles was a "semi Grandee," Al says, "who had quote married beneath him and been disinherited and lived by his wits. I used to visit his wife and his little child in their drab apartment. José was a friend of Dos Passos and translated *Manhattan Transfer* into Spanish, and as a young intellectual he and Dos Passos and Alfred Cortot, the French pianist, had taken hiking trips through Spain."

Then there was "Mr. Vermont," as he called himself, a hard-bitten practical Belgian named Montvert who spoke four or five languages and confessed to his French class that when someone spoke to him he wasn't necessarily sure what language they were speaking. "We soon found" — this is Al talking — "that when translating into French for him, if we couldn't remember a certain word and inserted the Spanish word instead, or sometimes even the English word, he never noticed. This taught me that there is a lot of flexibility in language and that the main thing is to keep going and then you can get away with it. It was like the way Prossy plays the piano. She would make fluffs but she wouldn't stop."

The most revered man at Hopkins in Al's day was Woodrow Wilson, who had done some graduate work there forty-odd years before. The boys used to guess on how often their history teacher, Dr. Latané — his family summed up Baltimore: one brother was an Episcopal bishop and the other one was head of the Maryland State Racing Commission — would say in every class, "As I said to Woodrow . . ." High guesser usually won. A more popular professor was Broadus Mitchell, the southern economist, whose course was enjoyed partly because he said shocking things à la H. L. Mencken, and did shocking things like run for governor of the state on the Socialist ticket. He taught economics by reading the boys Dickens, and Al could go home and tell Minnie that Professor Mitchell said, "Jesus Christ was a joiner, he was a Beta" — Beta being the biggest fraternity on campus and looked down upon by the Alpha Delts as a noisy vulgar place where the fine art of drinking wasn't cultivated. There were eight hundred undergrads altogether — a third of the hundred and fifty seniors were "grimy" engineers, as the other two-thirds called them. Charlie Reese (a class behind) who looked up to Al — Charlie went into banking, was president of the Hopkins Alumni Association, and is now a special fund raiser for Hopkins — still remembers the dressing-down Al gave him when he said "shit." Al said it was not gentlemanly. And Charlie says he has never used the word since. Al, however, sure has, but he claims he only uses it because in the year he spent with Oliver Wendell Holmes, the justice twice said "shit." But then Al could intimidate Charlie, because

Charlie's mother kept telling him Al was going to be President of the United States and kept asking him why he couldn't be more like Al. In addition to getting engaged to a respectable girl at Hopkins, Al had a girlfriend named Colette, whose father was a streetcar motorman. He used to go over to her house and dance to swing records, but was understandably afraid to fuck her because her father was always in the next room. Donie had already started taking girls home to Minnie's when she was off on trips, and Al once took Colette home when the coast was clear, but nothing much happened, largely because she was dry and kept saying, "Hurry up."

Al wasn't circumcised until he was seventeen, and when he was five and supposed to be taking a nap, he was playing with himself and his foreskin got caught behind the head of his penis, which was extremely painful. His screams brought Minnie and all the women in the family into his room, but they couldn't do anything and had to send for the doctor five miles away in St. Michaels. Al didn't play with himself after that — one of the few real tragedies of his life. He did make sure that I was circumcised at birth.

Despite all his achievements as an undergraduate, Al did not win the Alexander K. Barton Cup, awarded for outstanding character and leadership and named for a young minister who died from blood poisoning after he cut himself changing a diaper, because at the last performance of *Bunker Bean*, Al's pals substituted real gin for the water martinis he quaffed in the final scene, and Al went off and dropped a whitewashed stone on the marble steps in front of the main building, which were still pristine, because the suburban Hopkins campus was then only ten years old. The university itself was fifty years old. It was famous for its graduate and medical schools and as the place where saccharin was developed. The repair can still be seen in the steps — for some years it was the only memorial to Alger at Hopkins because after he got into a jam with the

Feds, the university, which in 1947 had given him an honorary LL.D, expunged his academic record. He's now back on the rolls, but his name is still missing from the Alpha Delt roster. Donie won the Barton Cup three years after Al graduated. Al 'fessed up to the broken step after he sobered up, which was why he got into a jam with the deans. They gave the Barton Cup to a teetotaling athlete who later hit the bottle and died of cancer.

The "Statistics of the Senior Class" in Al's yearbook list Al as the most popular man in his class, one of the eight men who have done most for their alma mater, runner-up (by one vote) as Most Prominent in Student Activities, winner as Best All-Around Man, runner-up as Most Perfect Gentleman, second place again as Leading Politician: "The biggest and best hand shaker is Alger Hiss, who holds forth in the Tudor and Stuart Rooms." The only categories Al did not place in were Best Student, Best Athlete, Best Dressed Man, Biggest Snake, Collegiate Specimen, and Leading Barnhound.

The three favorite women's colleges were Goucher, Vassar, and Smith. There were more Democrats than Republicans, there were also a couple of Socialists — this was attributed to Broadus Mitchell's influence — Lucky Strikes were the favorite cigarette, the *Baltimore Sun* was the favorite newspaper, and the three most popular authors were H. L. Mencken, Mark Twain, and James Branch Cabell. Dr. Wight was the most popular professor. The majority of the class said they only wanted to have two children, and only ten men in the class of '26 said they didn't neck. The class tabulated the daily dozen vices in the same order the previous class had: cheating, stealing, lying, sex irregularity, snobbishness, gambling, selfishness, vulgar talk, drinking, laziness, extravagance, and dancing.

Alger, whose favorite authors at the time were Saki, Shaw, Max Beerbohm, and Heywood Broun — whose column in

the New York *World* he read daily — was singled out by the
yearbook as "a shining success" who "has the real stuff," "the
epitome of success," and "our nominee for Mr. Hopkins."
"He goes in for culture, and activities are his sideline. Judging
solely by the extent of his sideline, Alger must be the most
cultured, learned bozo around this neck of the woods." "Like
Socrates, we admit our ignorance in the face of his irresistible
logic and rhetoric. To all of which we add the usual pat on
the back, but this time it does not nauseate us to give it:
Alger is a nice chappie in spite of his attainments."

A recent letter from a classmate, A. Risley Ensor, who
teaches law at the University of Baltimore — he invented a
popular Collegiate Cab Contest at Hopkins: top prize went
to the most dilapidated vehicle entered — says, "As were
most students I was conscious of the magnetic presence of
Alger Hiss. Not all of us mature at the same rate. In your
father's case I believe that he entered Hopkins as a mature
person acutely aware of the world beyond the campus. It is
not surprising then that by the time he graduated from Harvard Law School he was ready to assume a role of national
leadership.

" 'Was he a happy kid?' 'Or was he a serious young fellow?'
I believe he was both. Only a happy person could have won
the universal affection of his fellow students. Only a serious
one could have engendered the admiration and respect of his
contemporaries."

Al went to Europe the summer before his junior year — it
was the first summer steamship lines had ever offered cheap
rates for students — and on board ship, while reading Proust,
he met a girl, Priscilla Fansler, who had just graduated from
Bryn Mawr, not one of the three most popular colleges among
the class of '26 at Hopkins, but one with a reputation for
brainy girls. He was nineteen and she was twenty.

She was demure and pretty, and her plans for the summer

seemed uncertain — she talked vaguely about living in a sleeping bag on the south downs of England. This made Al feel "worldly wise" and "avuncular," and he and three or four other guys on the boat, similarly affected by this dame, went off and took rooms for a while at a boarding house in Kensington Square the Fansler girl had heard about until they were sure she could take care of herself. He saw her again at the end of the summer — took her down to Southampton to put her on her boat — and when he got home again he started corresponding with her because he had met her under romantic circumstances. She wrote she couldn't understand how he could stand being in ROTC, and he wrote back that when he heard the band playing "The Star-Spangled Banner" he felt very patriotic, and didn't she feel exactly the same way?

Al's theory about marriage at this time, even though he later got himself engaged in college to a southern girl, was that it stood in a man's way and restricted his freedom, and he thought marriage had not been of much use in making his parents happy. So he had decided never to get married — "unless absolutely necessary" — meaning unless he found himself in a circumstance where both he and some girl couldn't live without each other.

The next winter, when the Fansler girl was a grad student in English at Yale, she came down to Baltimore to visit a Yalie who lived in the Linden Avenue neighborhood, Dudley Digges. Dudley Digges's mother told Minnie the girl was "boy-crazy." One night the girl, Dudley, Al, and some others all went off to a dance in a taxi. The Fansler girl sat on Al's lap, and he suddenly discovered, for the first time, that she turned him on — at which moment she announced she'd just gotten engaged to another man, a Yalie named Thayer Hobson. The following spring, she did marry this other guy, went off to Paris, had a son, came back to New York, he divorced her, she had an affair, she got pregnant, she had an abortion, and after all of this, five years later, Al turns up again, still single, and she tells him he can stick around if he'll marry her right away, so they get married in December 1929.

It happened like this. In the spring of '29, when Al was about to graduate law school, a pal named Bill Vodrey said he was going to New York with his girl to see *Parsifal* and didn't Al have a girl? Al had just heard that Priscilla Hobson was divorced, which sounded racy, so he wrote her, and she invited him to spend the weekend at her place. He thought he had it made in the shade and went out and bought a diaphragm. But it turned out there was another guy hanging around the gay divorcée's apartment, and when Al got her alone and mentioned the diaphragm, she laughed and said you had to be fitted for diaphragms and he was just a "virgin boy" and she wouldn't sleep with him because she already had a boyfriend. Al took her to *Parsifal* anyway. In the summer he went off to Europe with Donie, who got an ulcer in France. When Al got home, Mrs. Hobson met the boat. By now Al felt he had fallen for her "hook, line, and sinker." In the meantime, she had gotten pregnant, but her boyfriend wouldn't marry her because his wife got pregnant immediately afterward. So she had an abortion. When Al got back, she went into the hospital for an operation for a tipped uterus — to cure the pains in her side. (It didn't.) He called her at the hospital and told her he couldn't live without her. She told him she wasn't interested in an affair, only marriage. And that's how mom and dad got together. Mom told dad about the abortion some years later.

A few words about Priscilla Harriet Fansler Hobson Hiss, called "Pros" or "Prossy," or, by her mother, Willia Spruill Fansler, "Pritsy Pru." Prossy never talked much to me about her childhood, and never mentioned her mother. Both her parents died before I was born. She has a picture of her dad, which she used to show me — the picture shows a good-

looking guy with a neatly trimmed full beard — and I can
remember her sometimes telling me that he had been a wonderful man, that the Spruills were kin to a crème de la crème
family in Kentucky named DeRespass, that one of her
brothers had taken to drink, that brothers Dean and Tommy
were good and brothers Ralph and Henry mean, that she had
driven the family around in their old car when she was still
a teen-ager. When I was a teen-ager and got drunk she used
to tell me not to or I'd turn into an alcoholic. But she also
used to tell me — after we moved to New York — not to talk
with a Brooklyn accent or else I'd never be able to stop. Both
she and Alger talk what I'd call cultured East Coast, well-
modulated with good diction and no regionalisms. This I
picked up from them very good. New York cab drivers still
ask me — and I've lived here twenty-eight years — "You
from out of town?" New Yorkers sometimes tell me I'm
from Boston. Bostonians guess Philadelphia.

Prossie's dad, Tom Fansler, was born in topsoil-rich farmland — Macoupin County, in southern Illinois — in 1854.
He wrote down his own story and the story of his dad — "A
True Story of an Illinois Farmer" — at the age of eighty-
three. In the spring of 1852 Tom's dad, twenty-five years old,
put his wife and his first two sons and everything they owned
on a raft he had built and left east Tennessee for the Illinois
country. Reports had come over the Cumberland Mountains
that there was good farmland up there. The raft floated down
the Tennessee to where it joins the Ohio at Paducah, and
then floated down the Ohio to where it joins the Mississippi
at Cairo. There he sold the raft for passage on a steam packet
up the river to Alton, Illinois, where he trekked inland and
built a one-room log cabin amid the wide prairies. He had
fifty dollars in his pocket at the time and took a job making
rails, at the rate of one dollar per hundred rails. Fifteen
years later he had a hundred-and-twenty-acre farm, and by

the time he died in 1897 he had 240 acres and had sent most of his kids to college. "His agricultural philosophy," Tom wrote, "was that it always pays to give back to the soil a little more than you take out." He did this by raising corn, buying cattle and hogs, feeding grain to the animals and then selling them and using their manure on his land. "In all his long life, I never knew my father to sell a bushel of corn other than in well-fatted cattle and hogs."

Two pages of Tom Fansler's book-length memoir are given over to a paraphrase of "Acres of Diamonds," a Chautauqua lecture delivered some 6000 times by Dr. Russell H. Conwell, founder of Temple University in Philadelphia. The lecture is the story of the Persian Al Hafed, a happy farmer with a huge spread, money at interest, a beautiful wife and lovely kids, who abandons everything when an old priest tells him, "If you want diamonds, all you have to do is go look for them, and when you find them, you will have them." Al winds up in Spain dead broke and starving while the guy who takes over his farm makes a fortune working Al's gorgeous land — the "acres of diamonds which the old Persian had overlooked." Tom then draws the moral: "We say to the sober, industrious farmers of these great American Commonwealths — keep your farms with all diligence, and your farms will keep you."

There is no mention in this "true story" of Tom's mom, except when he calls her "the good wife and mother" who died before his father and when he says that both his parents had brothers who fought on both sides of the Civil War. What Prossy's dad does say is: "Former President Calvin Coolidge said many things during his all too brief lifetime, but nothing finer than in these words, 'If we could surround ourselves with forms of beauty, the evil things of life would tend to disappear and our moral standards would be raised.' " Another quote from Tom: "The most significant discovery any young person can make is to discover his own powers and limitations . . . A knowledge of one's limitations will or may restrain him from attempting the impossible in which fruitless tasks, vitality and substance are drained and scattered." When Tom was a boy, the grass in Macoupin County grew so tall that if he wanted to see the cows he'd been sent to fetch home for milking he had to get on horseback.

Tom grew up to be a schoolteacher. Enter Willia Spruill, named for her dad, a Louisville preacher.

Willia is the feminine of William. She married the happy young schoolteacher and quickly motivated him into the insurance business and successive moves to Evanston, Illinois, outside of Chicago, and Fraser, Pennsylvania, near the Main Line outside of Philadelphia, where Willia and Thomas bought an old farmhouse they called "Roadside Acres," the name coming from the first line of a popular poem of the time: "Let me build a house by the side of the road / Where the race of men go by." Thomas was a good-looking guy with a beard who liked to garden. He didn't talk much — his wife complained that Fansler men liked to retreat into stony silence — and in his later years he grew increasingly deaf. Willia talked a lot. She was an Anglophile and held academic achievement in high esteem, especially Ph.D.s and college professors. She was a large strong woman built something like Minnie Hiss. When one of her daughters-in-law brought a friend into Willia's Pennsylvania kitchen one day for presentation, Willia stared over the woman's head in stony silence. At lunch she was gracious to the woman, and after lunch she bawled out the daughter-in-law — "I *never* receive in the kitchen."

Thomas and Willia had eight kids over a span of about twenty years. Two died young. The six who survived were Dean, Daisy, Ralph, Henry, Tommy, and Prossy. Prossy, the baby, was born in Evanston on October 13, 1903. The

Fanslers moved to Pennsylvania ten years later. Willia's two favorite children were Dean and Pritsy Pru, Dean because he got a Ph.D. in medieval studies and married a Ph.D. and Pritsy Pru because she was pretty, smart, and the baby. Willia sang a lullaby to Pritsy Pru that went:

> Go 'way Dean
> And go 'way Daisy,
> Go 'way Ralph
> And go 'way Henry —
> Pritsy Pru is mama's baby,
> Pritsy Pru is mama's love!

Tommy, who was named for his father, didn't even make it into the song. Ralph and Henry, a dozen or so years older than P.P., used to tell her, "Die the death of a rag doll."

Dean and his wife, Harriet, taught at the University of Manila for some years and for a few years tried to start a chicken farm in Connecticut, Harriet reasoning, as she said, "If a farmer can get five dollars from a chicken, two Ph.Ds ought to be able to get twenty-five dollars."

All the kids were bright, but none of the others turned into professors. Ralph became a bank examiner, but wrote a biography of Walt Whitman. Henry had charm, played the violin, went into advertising, and liked to drink. Daisy became head music librarian in Philadelphia. As a young woman she affected a drawl, called people "honey-chile," and told them her name was not Fansler, really, but Van Rensselaer. She never married. Dean and Harriet went back to the Philippines just before World War II — Dean was made a dean — and were caught there when the Japanese moved in. The last message he was able to get out was a telegram to his daughter Pritsy — "OK SO FAR" — a reference to his favorite joke, the one about the man who falls off the Empire State

Building. As he passes the fiftieth floor a friend asks him how he's doing . . .

During the occupation, Dean's students smuggled him an egg a week. Harriet died, and after that Dean, who spoke all the Philippine dialects, went to work for the underground and had a ball. He survived the war, but only by a few months.

Tommy thought of becoming a medical student, went into medieval studies but never completed his Ph.D. thesis about the medieval image of Hell Mouth, and in his later years was director of the National Safety Council and wrote unpublished novels. He was four years older than Prossy and she was devoted to him. Willia, who occasionally, it is said, adopted a tone of unctuous scorn, employed it one time to describe Tommy. "He was always my *good* boy." His first wife was an art historian and his second wife was a buyer for a Chicago department store. At the age of fifty-nine he had a prostate operation and was given a clean bill of health. The next year, at a moment when all three of his daughters happened to be pregnant, he committed suicide. Prossy used to tell people he committed suicide because he knew he had inoperable cancer. The religious tradition in the family was soap-swimming Presbyterianism, which meant if you went swimming you always took a cake of soap along so you wouldn't waste your time.

Prossy had many talents. People said her only problem was deciding how to use her talents. She played the piano well, she drew well, she sang well, and she was good in school. Willia sent her to the Phoebe Anna Thorne Model Open Air Day School for Girls, an experimental school in Bryn Mawr that held classes outdoors, and to Bryn Mawr College, where Prossy majored in philosophy and went to lots of dances at Haverford.

As a freshman Pritsy Pru started palling around with Justine Wise, daughter of the famous reform rabbi, and liked to go to Sunday dinners at the Wise home. In her junior year she and a girlfriend she went to dances with moved to a dorm, where Prossy introduced herself to Roberta Murray and her best friend and told them she thought they were the brightest girls in school. And then she got to know all the Murrays — her friends said she liked to "adopt" new families periodically. Later she introduced Bobbie Murray, a bright art student from an old New York Quaker family that had given its name to Murray Hill, to her favorite brother, Tommy. Tommy and Bobbie hit it off and got married a year later, and Prossy liked to tell Bobbie that she had arranged the marriage. She also adopted the habit of calling people close to her "thee" instead of "you" in the Quaker tradition.

Prossy threw over her first boyfriend, her second boyfriend threw her over, and there's some confusion about the third boyfriend. Prossy was carrying with her on the boat to Europe where she met Al one of Bobbie's guidebooks to England. When Prossy returned it the next fall Bobbie was surprised to discover that she had used one of the blank pages at the back of the book as a diary, writing that she loved a man in England named Judd Chambers, that she didn't know how to tell him about it, but that somehow she knew that if he weren't married he would want her. Judd Chambers was a friend of Bobbie's and had always given Bobbie to understand that if he wasn't married and she wasn't either, he'd be interested in her.

Prossy went to Yale graduate school the next year in English, and there she met Thayer Hobson, a Yale classmate and fellow Skull and Bones member of Henry Luce's and Brit Hadden's, the co-founders of *Time*. A brother of Thayer's later became Episcopal bishop of southern Ohio. Thayer was the B.M.O.C. at Yale at that point and was married to the daughter of Walter Camp, the famous Yale football coach. He ducked off to France to divorce her so he could marry Prossy, and after the two of them were hitched he took Prossy off to Paris and set her up in a big apartment, and Prossy bossed around a large staff of French servants. The next year they took a place on the Upper East Side of Manhattan, and Timmy was born in order to cure the recurring stitch in Prossy's side. She'd been getting cramps in her side for years — Al had first noticed it when walking around London with her in the summer of '24. But having the baby didn't do the trick.

Thayer left after another year for another woman, and Harry Luce gave Prossy a job on his new magazine, *Time*. She was office manager there for a year and wrote Letters to the Editor when the readers didn't send in enough. She still has a letter from Harry offering her a recommendation at any time for any job. After that Prossy went to Columbia and finished her M.A. in English. One night she took a long walk with her sister-in-law, Bobbie, and told Bobbie she didn't see why she should divorce Thayer because she still wanted to live with him even though he didn't want to live with her. Thayer got a Mexican divorce and married Laura Zametkin, who became famous in the forties, as Laura Z. Hobson, when she wrote *Gentlemen's Agreement,* a novel about anti-Semitism among upper-class WASPs.

I've met Laura, because her adopted son, Christopher Z. Hobson, was a classmate of mine at Harvard, and I eventually met Thayer, who was by then a happily retired publisher with a nice spread in Texas — he had been head of William Morrow and Company for many years — and his fourth wife at Tim's wedding in 1961. He was a nice old man. For years Al thought Thayer was "an ogre" for having, as Prossy told him, abandoned her, although he gave her child support. After Al's indictment Thayer turned out to be very helpful — one of Whit Chambers' famous stories to the House Committee on Un-American Activities was that Al had boasted he was such a dutiful Commie he had given money Thayer had sent him for Tim's schooling to the Communist Party and had sent Timmy to a cheaper school. What Al had done was put Tim in a more expensive school, and when Thayer had kicked up a fuss, Al made up the difference, to the tune of several hundred dollars a year. "I knew the son of a bitch was a liar when I heard that one," Thayer said of Chambers, confirming Al's version. Al later got mad at Thayer for being "stand-off-ish on Tim" after he heard about Tim's having said he'd been gay — Thayer wouldn't give Tim any dough when he went off to med school in Switzerland in the fifties — but then was pleased again when Thayer and Tim got to be friends after Tim had made a success of himself. Thayer left Tim a third of his estate when he died in the middle sixties.

Al married Prossy right in the middle of his year as law clerk to Supreme Court Justice Oliver Wendell Holmes. Holmes had a policy against this — his legal secretaries were supposed to postpone marriage plans until after their time with him — but Al didn't hear about that until the morning of his wedding, and anyway he hadn't thought about getting married when he'd taken the job in the spring. Holmes was gracious enough about it and offered Al two weeks off, but Alger and Prossy spent a weekend honeymoon on the Eastern Shore. Holmes wanted to give Al a check as a wedding present, but Al held out for a volume of the old man's speeches. Holmes inscribed the book "To Alger Hiss," and when Al told him he'd hoped for a longer inscription, the Justice added "et ux." — legal Latin for "and wife." Donie was best man at the wedding, and Minnie sent a telegram to Al that said, "DO NOT TAKE THIS FATAL STEP."

Al says he never had any sexual problems with Prossie until he got out of jail. "Sex was just quite joyous, and well worth waiting for. Of course, I thought I was extremely knowledgeable, I'd read Krafft-Ebing and Havelock Ellis and Marie

Stokes, and I had a considerable intellectual interest in the ramifications of sex, and I'd always thought that any normal young man, upon receiving the opportunity, could readily become as proficient as possible — and I was right. It wasn't that I had been saving myself for a good woman, it was a matter of the accidents of opportunity. If a lissome young lady had come along . . . Donie was a really talented swordsman. I made passes — they just didn't work. Promiscuity has always seemed to me a sign of confusion. That is more than a moralistic hang-up because I still have that view today. One is likely to be exploiting another person. That's why I never slept with that girl I knew in Cambridge while I was at Harvard. There would have been inequality in our positions. For me it would've been pure pleasure, but she was looking, I sensed, for something more lasting and important. I'm perfectly willing for people to be close, if there's equality. That may be a rationalization — but it's stayed with me. My great moral dread is that I might be exploiting people, morally, psychologically, or financially.

"I would prefer to be exploited. If I have to choose between the two, then I would rather be exploited."

Al went to Harvard Law School, partly because of his sister Mary Ann, who got him to talk to a friend of hers there, Professor Manley Hudson, who spent some months each year at The Hague as a judge on the World Court of Arbitration. Al still wanted to make a career in the foreign service and Hudson said law school would be excellent preparation. The rumor that was floating around Harvard when I was a student there in the sixties — namely that Alger Hiss had the highest marks of anyone who'd ever been to the law school — isn't true, but Al's marks were good enough to get him elected to the *Law Review* at the end of his freshman year, which meant he was in the top 1½ percent of his class. A third of the class was always dropped at the end of the freshman year, and everyone who was there in those days has a vivid memory of Professor "Bull" Warren saying at the first meeting of the year, "Gentlemen, look at the man on your right and the man on your left. Next year one of you three will be gone!"

Al says he studied hard for two years, which meant working nights and weekends, and coasted a little his third year. By the time he graduated he had decided to be a lawyer. Charley Horsky, who ran into him a couple of years later at the Department of Justice, where they were both working in the solicitor general's office, calls Al "a premier lawyer" — Horsky's now counsel for the Southern Railway and for the trustees of the Penn Central: "He has the prime ingredients: he's a good scholar, in touch with history, an excellent brief writer, he's articulate, has brains, and a winning personality that is not abrasive."

The man with the highest marks in Al's class was Tommy Austern. Some of the members of the *Law Review* wanted Al to run for the job. To Al it seemed clear that they didn't want Austern, a Jew, elected. But Al, who remembers being "self-consciously and a bit priggishly pro-Semitic," addressed the membership meeting and told them he thought he was being put up just to keep Austern out of it and that Austern had worked hard, slaved, and deserved it. The two candidates left the room and Austern won.

Since he wasn't going to be president, Al decided not to accept any other title on the *Law Review*, thus giving himself time to coast some his last year. So his classmate Lee Pressman became Notes Editor and his classmate Ed McLean became Case Notes Editor. Pressman later worked for the Triple A (the Agricultural Adjustment Administration), the first New Deal agency Al worked for, and there joined a small Marxist studies group, which, according to the engaging con man Whit Chambers, Al and Donie also belonged to, and which, according to Pressman, Donie, and Al, they didn't.

Anyway, Pressman gave Al an assignment to write a note for the *Law Review* about Yellow Dog contracts, and Al, who had never looked into labor law before, got interested and wrote a piece saying he thought labor had been screwed during the twenties. Ed McLean, later a federal judge, was one of the lawyers who defended Al against Chambers' scam.

One of the two letters of introduction Al came armed to Cambridge with was to Dr. Harvey Cushing, the famous Boston surgeon, so he took tea with the doctor and his Mrs. and their three girls, the famous Cushing sisters, Mary, Betsy, and Babs. Betsy was going out with Jimmy Roosevelt, married him, then divorced him and married John Hay Whitney. Al tried to promote something between Mary and his classmate Dick Field, but she married Vincent Astor and later James Fosburgh. Babs got hitched to Bill Paley, head of CBS. Mary Ann, Al's glamorous sister, who had been threatening suicide for years, finally went through with it a month before Al graduated law school, during final exams. Bosley had kicked the bucket a couple of months after Al arrived at law school.

Al was taken up by Professor Felix Frankfurter, who was always on the lookout for a half-dozen of the most promising and prepossessing, so that meant he often got to go to tea at the Frankfurters' on Sundays and listen to Felix, who was charming, whose mind was fast, who could talk brilliantly on any subject of current interest, and whose secret was a fantastic memory. Al was on full scholarship all three years at Harvard — and all four years at Hopkins, too, after the first term.

Al was planning to clerk for a federal judge in Maryland the year after law school when he got a letter from the hero of Harvard, Oliver Wendell Holmes, Jr., inviting him to be his law clerk in Washington. So at the age of twenty-four Al went to work for a living. Holmes was an eighty-eight-year-old man whose wife had just died; he'd been a captain in the Civil War and he'd been on the United States Supreme Court for twenty-seven years. The letter said, "Of course, you must understand that at my age I reserve the right to resign or die," but Al later found out that he'd been writing that to every clerk since he joined the Court at the age of sixty-one. Felix Frankfurter, in consultation with his wife, Marion, chose a Harvard graduate for Holmes every year. "A young man of promise," as Al says, "if that's not immodest in my case." Holmes's clerk of the year reported to work on the Friday before the first Monday in October — the Monday being the day the court went back to work. The clerk was paid $3600 for the year by the government, he worked in the judge's study in his town house on I Street in Georgetown, writing down the names of all the cases that came before the court in a docket the judge kept, as well as notes about all the briefs submitted. The clerks also briefed the judge about the facts and arguments in "the bloody certs" (Holmes pun: petitions for certiorari, i.e., review, by the Supreme Court). Holmes then flipped through the briefs submitted with the certs, to see if the clerks knew what they were talking about, took a few notes, and then made up his mind on the spot whether he'd vote to accept the case at the Court's next judicial conference.

Holmes called his clerks "sonny" when he was in a good mood and "idiot boy" when he was angry at them. As a boss, Al says, Holmes was "marvelous, fearsome, because he was exacting and expected you to produce your best, which you were only too happy to do. You couldn't flag, because you weren't there that long and anyway you didn't want to miss a minute of it. The intellectual excitement of being with him was just extraordinary." Holmes's clerks all adored him and Alger and Donie — Donie clerked for Holmes three years after Alger, the only brothers who ever served as Holmes's clerks — both remember him more vividly than anyone else they ever met, and they both talk about him at the drop of a hat in a way they won't talk about anybody else except Cory Roberts. "Holmes and Cory were the only two uninhibited people I'd ever met," Al says, when I tell him he gets a glow in his tone whenever the talk turns their way. "It was a celestial time with Holmes, and Donie and I got to be in the choir." Holmes retired from the bench the year before Donie worked for him, but Donie said, "I'll serve Justice Holmes on or off the Court and learn more law just talking to him." Donie got to Harvard the year after Al left and hated Felix for a while because Felix's first remark to him was, "Ah, a blond Alger!"

Al talked Holmes into letting him spend a summer at the judge's farm in Beverly, Massachusetts, the first clerk to do that, partly to keep the widower from getting lonely and partly just to hang around some more. Al also conned Holmes through what he calls a "benign conspiracy" to let Al read aloud to him for two or three hours in the evenings after work, something only Holmes's wife had done previously. Holmes was gruff when Al suggested the idea on several occasions, so Al got one of the judge's friends, Sir Esme Howard, the British ambassador to Washington, to tell Holmes how much he enjoyed having his son read aloud to him. That clinched the deal.

Al read Horace Walpole's letters to the judge, seven whole volumes, as well as P. G. Wodehouse and E. Phillips Oppenheim thrillers. "Well, what should it be this time?" Holmes would ask Al. "Shall we improve our minds or shall we have a little murder?" Sherlock Holmes was not on the judge's reading list. Holmes always went to sleep, but invariably snapped to if Al stopped for a minute. "Why did you stop? Go on. Did you think I missed something? Did you think I wasn't listening?" Al says he never dared say, "Because you were snoring slightly." And he later found out that none of the clerks who followed him — Holmes died in 1935 — ever dared say it either. Holmes died of pneumonia at home on I Street. His last visitor was Frankfurter, to whom he couldn't talk because he was in an oxygen tent. So he put his thumb on his nose and wiggled his fingers at Frankfurter. Holmes was twenty-three years older than Al and Donie's dad, Charlie, and nineteen years younger than Charlie's dad, who had been dead for eighteen years before either one of them was born. When I was a kid, from all the talk, I used to think Holmes was my grandfather.

Here's Al talking about Justice Holmes: "He was probably the most handsome man I have ever seen. He had marvelous swirling mustachios, white, plenty of hair, all white, very blue eyes, lovely coloring, lovely ruddy cheeks, and a gorgeous voice. He had this marvelous ringing laugh, as Roosevelt did. When Lady Pollock, the wife of his old friend, Sir Fred Pollock, the legal historian, both in their eighties, said at dinner at Beverly one night about another friend, 'She's feeling her years — she's eighty-four or eighty-five,' Holmes leaned back in his chair and with a great roar of laughter said, 'Oh, what's eighty among adults?' And Priscilla and I — who were both there to give the illusion of a big dinner party for the Pollocks — our ages added together would have been half of anyone's there. But it was so natural and spontaneous. He had a slight stoop, but four years later when Donie was there, and President Roosevelt four days after his first inauguration called on him on his ninety-second birthday without any publicity about it, just the opposite of the way a President would do something now, the judge straightened up like the old soldier he was to his full six feet, and greeted the President as his commander-in-chief. The President asked him whether he, the Justice, had any words for him, and he said, 'Form your battalions and fight, sir.'

"One day I showed him pictures in a glossy magazine of the first international beauty contest. I remember one comment: 'Oh, I could toy with her for the odd half-hour.' It was a sight to be at the breakfast table and watch him eat. He peeled an orange first — he liked to see if he could get it all off in one strip. Then oatmeal, and then he had a poached egg on toast with an absolute mat of anchovy paste from S.S. Pierce in Boston between the egg and the toast. I remember him saying one time that if all the steaks and chops and roasts that had been consumed in his house were packed in boxcars that would be a long, long line of food. He had very good taste in everything.

"Justice Harlan Fiske Stone would come up to the second floor of the house where Holmes's desk and my desk were, and Holmes would take out the big portfolios with his collection of prints and etchings and he and Stone would pore over them with a glass, and Holmes would point out which were first states and which were second states. And Stone, who had been attorney general and before that dean of the Columbia Law School, was like a little boy with his teacher. One night Charlie Willard, my roommate before Prossie and I got married, and I took him and a couple of attractive girls to see the Marx Brothers on the stage. We sat in a box, and afterward the judge had us all back to 1720 I Street for tea. One of the girls said she knew someone in the show and Holmes said, 'Could you have taken me backstage? And you come here and take my tea? Oh, young lady. Young lady!' "

Al could talk for hours about Holmes, so let's let him go on for a while: "He liked champagne — the bubbly as he called it — and was a great fancier of Churchill-sized S.S. Pierce Havana cigars. When he was working at his standing writing desk, clouds of beautiful smoke would circle around his beautiful head. It wasn't illegal to drink during prohibition, it was just illegal to sell liquor, so friends would bring him bottles of champagne and he would always say, even though champagne doesn't keep very long, 'I take judicial notice that this is pre-Prohibition stock.' And then he would say, 'Don't answer. Don't answer.' He had enough Scotch in his cellar to last a long time. The bookshelves in the big room on the second floor ran from floor to ceiling. He read to himself as well. When I was with him he was reading Thucydides in the original — my Greek wasn't that good. 'When I appear before *Le Bon Dieu*,' he said, 'He may say to me, "Holmes, can you recite on Thucydides?" If I have to say, "No, Sire," think what a fool I'd feel.'

"Holmes was a well-filled-out person with a good paunch, not a protuberant paunch, but a man of solidity, and enough flesh on his face so that he certainly wasn't gaunt. Brandeis looked almost gaunt — Roosevelt's name for him was the Prophet Isaiah — his hair was sort of Einsteinian, and when you went to dinner at Brandeis' house you seldom got enough to eat. What you were served was tasty, but the portions were sparing because he himself ate sparingly.

"One time when I went to the Brandeis' for dinner with my wife, it must have been in the spring because we were served asparagus; as a farm boy from Maryland I not only liked asparagus, I was accustomed to eating heartily of it. I remember that Senator Burton Wheeler was also a guest. There was lively discussion on politics and international topics, and very little wit. Brandeis did not believe in waste so his waiter was his Supreme Court messenger, a pale old black man named Poindexter, very sweet, very frail and tiny, and he was not a disciplined or experienced waiter, otherwise he would not have served me first. I helped myself to asparagus, and I noticed he seemed to pale even more. And I didn't know what was wrong until I realized that there wasn't any more asparagus in the kitchen. When the platter got to Senator Wheeler, there was one stalk left."

Holmes's house in the country was a small house on the main street of a small town. It had a small cluttered living room and a big long dining room looking out on the garden. His town house was a brownstone in downtown Washington; the room he and Al worked in there was a second-floor study with high ceilings and the walls completely lined with books. It had an overstuffed armchair for Holmes, his desk, and also his standing desk where he wrote his opinions — he said that standing to write kept him succinct — and there was also a desk for the secretary. Holmes had four servants, a cook, Annie, a young Irish maid, Mary Cokely, who sassed him, a driver, Charlie Buckley, and his Supreme Court messenger, Thomas. Charlie had driven Holmes's carriage in the old days, and never got used to driving the judge's stately ancient Packard. Once when Holmes was out with Donie, Charlie almost hit a truck and Holmes said, "My Lord, sonny! What a blow to jurisprudence if he'd killed both of us!" Charlie told the secretaries that the judge and his wife always flirted in the car and would kick each other under the lap robe. Mary, when she helped Holmes on with his coat, would tell him, "Straighten up — or you'll be an old man before your time!" The judge would tell her: "Goddammit! Shut up!"

In the fall Al shared a luxurious bachelor flat with Charlie Willard and the two of them hired a sophisticated young black cook and maid named Roxy. After Al got married in December, he initially moved into this flat with Prossy and Timmy, who was now three, and Charlie Willard went to the Racquet Club. Al and Prossy soon found a small house on 30th Street in Georgetown. Al got very little sleep after the move, because Timmy, whose bedroom was next door, would get on his rocking horse, Buster, every morning at five o'clock and try to ride it through the intervening wall, and Al thought it was inappropriate to take the rocking horse away from Tim. Holmes would take Al out for drives during the day and Al would nod off. Holmes always noticed. "Late party last night, eh?" he would ask. Al wouldn't correct him.

Holmes learned in the Civil War that doubters were as brave as believers, that poor men without advantages were often better leaders of men than Harvard grads. "The generation that carried on the war has been set apart by its experience," he said in a Memorial Day speech he made in 1884. "Through our great good fortune, in our youth our hearts were touched with fire. It was given to us to learn at the outset that life is a profound and passionate thing."

The judge was also pleased by continuity. He had a Queen Anne mirror in Washington (left to Al in his will), which had once hung in his grandmother's house on Beacon Hill. The house had been commandeered by Lord Howe for the headquarters of his force during the Revolutionary War, and when Holmes was a boy his grandmother had told him that as a little girl she had seen the British troops march into Boston. "All the secretaries," Al says, "imbibed a tremendous sense of the continuity of history. We were all part of one woven strip, the great span. Sometimes Holmes would look roguishly into his grandmother's mirror. It was pretty murky by that time because the glass had never been changed, and he would say, 'Sonny, as I look in that mirror, I sometimes think I see the bewigged face of Lord Howe. Do you see him? Do you see him?' Holmes had once met someone in his youth, I don't know who, an elderly person, who in turn met someone who had actually met Peregrine White. Peregrine White was the baby born on the *Mayflower* in Cape Cod Bay, and he lived to a ripe old age. Holmes was very pleased that there were only two gaps between him and Peregrine White."

In a conversation recorded for the Columbia Oral History

Project, Al refers to Holmes's interest in the continuity of history as "an intellectual game." In other conversations Al takes the matter more seriously.

And there was the story about the cockroach. Holmes thought that as a householder he should inspect his premises periodically. His wife, Fanny, thought this was stupid and none of his business. One night Holmes went down into the kitchen, opened the flour barrel, and spied a roach. He lunged for it and flour went all over him and the kitchen. It was a rubber roach left there by Fanny. Fanny couldn't have children, so the couple never had any.

The only bawdy stories Al likes to tell are Holmes stories, like when Mrs. Curtis, a most proper Bostonian, came to call and the old man came downstairs with his fly open. When Al discreetly asked him, "What do elephants do?" the judge zipped up his pants and said, "I don't think Mrs. Curtis would be happy if we let our banners hang out on our outer walls, do you?" And Holmes told Donic — whom he always called "a rebel," since Donie was from Maryland — that writing Supreme Court opinions was very much like peeing. "You apply a pressure, a very vague pressure, and out it comes." When Holmes was twenty-one he was left for dead after the Battle of Ball's Bluff in the Civil War, and at the age of eighty-eight, as Professor Paul Freund of the Harvard Law School, a Brandeis clerk, scouted by Frankfurter has said, "Holmes had no belief in panaceas and very little in sudden ruin." Al thinks Holmes liked Donie better than he did him.

4. New Deal
and Raw Deal

AL HATED the Depression, like almost everyone else, but it improved his job opportunities. There's always plenty of work for movie stars and lawyers in a depression. And Al started to rise rapidly in the two law firms he worked for from '30 to '33, because the Depression was bringing them so much business that youngsters for the first time had the opportunity to get into trial work and other exciting things without having to carry a senior partner's briefcase for ten years first. Al also immediately became a very valuable young fellow in Washington because, as constitutional scholars have pointed out, the Supreme Court in the first thirty-five years of this century was exercising more power than at any other time in our history, and in the early New Deal days it was throwing out Roosevelt's legislation left and right, and the Democrats wanted to draft cunningly-worded bills that couldn't be tromped on quite so easily.

Roosevelt also had a theory — if you imported young guys with brains and no experience you got more for your dollar.

When Al left Holmes in the summer of 1930 after the crash, he turned down a job in the antitrust division of the

Department of Justice, partly because Hoover was already beginning to look unappealing to young Democrats, partly because he could make better money in private practice, and partly because Prossy had just been working for the Wickersham Commission, a presidential commission looking into law enforcement, particularly with regard to Prohibition. Hoover was so sensitive about press criticism that Prossy had been given the job of reading all the papers every day and sending off to the White House every article that mentioned the President. So Al joined Choate, Hall & Stewart, one of the most prestigious firms in Boston, where tea was served every afternoon, in order, Al suspected, to get everyone to work later. He immediately was put to work on the Gillette case, an important suit arising out of the Depression, from which he picked up the incidental information that Gillette even then knew how to make stainless steel blades that would last three times as long as the blades they were marketing. One of the things young New Dealers admired about Roosevelt was that he had a strop and would resharpen his old razor blades, and once boasted that he got twenty-seven shaves out of the same blade.

"Autostrop, a little company, a nothing company, but smart, had us over a barrel," as Al puts it. Gillette had for years been putting down on its books as sales any shipment of inventory to its wholly owned subsidiaries. After the crash, when the inventories stopped moving, this started to look like double-entry bookkeeping and Autostrop was suing the company and the board of directors for mismanagement. After the crash some of the directors had also started using company money to buy company stock just to keep the price up. Choate, Hall & Stewart was representing two of the directors, the president of American Optical, a rising Massachusetts firm, and the president of the First National Bank of Boston. The case was eventually settled out of court —

Autostrop got control of Gillette and nine million bucks —
but Al says if it hadn't been for negotiations, the settlement
would have been for twenty-three million. Al went to work
for $3600 a year and was hired to take the place of Archibald
MacLeish who had been there only a year or two and was
about to, in an unprecedented move, be offered a partnership,
but who had, instead, quit to write poetry. Al's immediate
boss was a junior partner named Max Foster, a friend of
MacLeish's and I. A. Richards', who later got in touch with
Al when Al was working on the United Nations Charter, because Richards wanted to have the charter written in Basic
English. Max was a Yalie who always wore a hat to cover a
bald spot, and had a full-length portrait of himself in his bedroom in Topsfield, Massachusetts, nude except for a hat. His
son, P. V. Foster, who was a schoolmate of mine at Putney
in Vermont, always wore a hat too.

Max introduced Al to "birding." A goldfinch hopped into
Max's living room one afternoon when he and Al were working there, and Max handed Al binoculars. "I was amazed," Al
says — "a bright, beady black eye, a bright golden creature,
and I was right on top of it." Al went out and bought a pair
of army surplus binoculars, which he still has, and he introduced Prossy to birding, which she still does. This got him
into trouble later because one of the things Chambers told
Nixon he remembered about Al was that Al had seen a
prothonotary warbler, a big item for a birder, and Nixon, who
had never heard of a prothonotary warbler, thought that
Chambers would have had to have been an intimate pal to
have come by this information.

Prossy loathed Cambridge, where she and Al and Timmy
had their nest, and bitched about it, and Al realized he had a
"sulky wife" on his hands. "When people around me are unhappy, I'm unhappy, and I wanted to make her happy. And
at the same time, I could see myself spending the rest of my

life summering on the North Shore or the Cape and getting stodgy." So when the same man who had offered him a job in the Justice Department quit the government to join a big Wall Street firm and offered Al a job there, Al accepted. "My sense of loyalty prevented me from leaving until the Gillette case was wrapped up, so I commuted to New York on weekends for six months." Prossy immediately moved down to New York with Timmy and took a railroad flat near Columbia and on the same floor with Bobbie and Tommy and helped the Socialist Party of Morningside Heights organize a soup kitchen. The apartment had bedbugs as well as roaches. But after Al got to town for good, she found a place on upper Central Park West overlooking the park and Al bought a cocker spaniel pup named Jenny for Tim because he thought boys should have dogs.

At his new firm, Cotton, Franklin, Wright & Gordon, Al was immediately put to work on another big case, the RCA case, by "Fafa" Gordon — that's what his wife called him — the former Justice Department man. The lawyers got to work about ten and then worked to all hours and Al took the subway down to Wall Street and read the *New York Times*. He had switched to the *Times* from the New York *World* in law school because Felix Frankfurter had said that anyone who didn't read the *Times* was misinformed. Al still reads the *Times* faithfully. The RCA case was a big antitrust case. RCA had been set up as a manufacturing unit of GE, Westinghouse, AT&T, and Western Electric, and the Justice Department wanted to split it up and distribute its patents. An elaborate deal was worked out splitting up RCA in this country and divorcing it from its parent companies but allowing it to maintain its working arrangements with the European cartel of manufacturers internationally. Raytheon got some RCA patents over here and that's how they got their start. Prossy was not sulky in New York and Al got a couple of raises and by the spring of '33 he was making $6000 a year, which was good money.

Al missed about 25 of the New Deal's famous First Hundred Days, because he didn't sign on until May '33. Jerome Frank, a big Wall Street lawyer, was going down to Washington as general counsel to the Agricultural Adjustment Administration, the New Deal's new Farm Agency, and wanted Al to come with him, but Al wanted to be pushed first. In the first chapter of his not yet finished book on the New Deal, Al says the push came in a telegram from Felix saying that "on basis national emergency" he had to take the job, and that this stilled "qualms I felt at abruptly pulling out of the work assigned to me."

"Frankfurter's peremptory call to duty was most welcome in that it disposed of any reason to delay," Al writes. "Words depreciate rapidly. In May 1933, 'National Emergency' was not a limp cliché. Even now, in the context of that telegram, the words stir me. They bring back the almost palpable feel of crisis. For in simple truth, the Great Depression had brought on a national emergency. A summons in Frankfurter's terms carried weight in most quarters, including the senior partners of most Wall Street law firms. I delayed no longer and went to Washington a few days later." By the time Al got to Washington, Roosevelt had already gotten the banks to reopen, and as Al puts it, "There came from the White House during the 'Hundred Days' a stream of messages to Congress recommending far-reaching legislation, proclamations and pronouncements that dwarf the opening months of all other administrations in our history. Walter Lippmann wrote on March fifteenth that in two weeks Roosevelt had accomplished a recapture of morale comparable to the 'second battle of the Marne' in the summer of 1916. A new America was in the making."

"The New Deal — it's amazing I ever got over it," Al said

the other day. "But then I've had other highlights too. Like the year with Holmes." Al says he left Washington in '47 with the same amount of money he came with, i.e., zilch. Al is not a saver. And he never earned over ten grand a year working for the government. And what he earned went on clothes, books, entertaining, a maid — who answered the phone, "Lawyer Hiss's residence," — concerts, a skating club, theater tickets. He rented houses in Washington, except in '43, during the war, when, with a loan from Minnie and a bank mortgage, he bought a small house in Georgetown for thirteen grand — there weren't any houses for rent during the war — and he bought one car during the Washington years, a '35 Plymouth, a dealer's model.

Al started at Agriculture at $6000 per, got a couple of raises up to $7000, then left Agriculture and went on the payroll of the Nye Committee, the Senate committee investigating the munitions industry, at $4500. The Nye Committee was in all the papers, but it had a tiny budget and since a couple of the senators were big agriculture men, they asked Al's boss for the loan of one of his boys, but after some months Al decided it wasn't fair that someone else should be doing his work at Agriculture without the title and the pay so he went on the congressional payroll. He's very proud of the fact that, as far as he knows, he's the only man except for Jimmie Byrnes who's worked for all three branches of the federal government. His next job was in the solicitor general's office in the Justice Department for $7000 and then he took a cut to $6500 to go to the State Department, where he got some raises up to $10,000. State was the only department that required its officers to join the Civil Service, and that is why Al now gets a government pension of $136 a month.

In law school Al decided to be a Renaissance man, and he read Frazer's *The Golden Bough* in bed every night for an hour before going to sleep. He had already read Proust, of course — and met Prossy as a consequence — and had tried to read Ouspensky. Al knew that Holmes, who as a youngster in Cambridge had palled around with Charles S. Peirce and Will and Harry James, and had thought of becoming a philosopher, believed it was possible to "live greatly in the Law." The boys in Alpha Delt and the Cane Club at Hopkins all had agreed that business was vulgar grubbing in money and that the only professions with cachet were, following the traditional English model, the church, the army, and the law, to which, because of Hopkins, they added medicine, it having been the aim of the Four Horsemen of Hopkins — the four most famous doctors in the country in their day — to write for medical journals in good English. One of the Four Horsemen, Popsy Welch, the great pathologist, was still alive at the time and hung around the Tudor and Stuart Club where, everyone was convinced, he was reading through the entire *Encyclopædia Britannica*. But Al, although he respected medicine, thought it was too difficult. The church and the army were sort of out of it, so it looked like it had to be diplomacy. But when he got to Harvard and fell in with Frankfurter, who had friends in Washington and London, and who popped off to Albany to consult with Governor Roosevelt, Al found out he was good at law and made the *Law Review*. This meant he had a chance to make friends with the faculty members, who didn't see much socially of the bottom 98.5 percent of the class. Al then decided law was O.K. Next he met Holmes, and Holmes was "a wide-angle-lens man."

Al also got, through associating with Frankfurter, who had tried to keep Sacco and Vanzetti alive, "politicized" at Harvard, which meant he decided that there were things that needed changing in the country, that there was a "vibrant, vigorous, strong American tradition of supporting the underdog," that "significant" reform was possible, that it was "supercilious and superficial" to think that all politicians were "dirty," as he had thought at Hopkins. Specifically, this meant that he got interested in what was then known as "the Movement," young labor leaders of the twenties who were trying to organize industry at a time when it was pretty impossible to do so. At Harvard Jim Landis, his rooming house landlady's nephew and later Dean of the Harvard Law School — he had to leave the deanery because he got involved with a married woman; he was a protégé of Joe Kennedy's, chairman of the SEC, and later of the Civil Aeronautics Board until he did something that pissed off Truman, and he went to jail for a little while for not filing his income tax returns — had just started teaching Harvard's first course in labor law. Prossy taught one summer, before she married Al, at a Bryn Mawr school designed to inculturate bright young union women, and she told Al when they married that she had been so disgusted when Al Smith lost to Hoover in '28 she had almost left the country for good.

In New York at Cotton and Franklin, after law school, Al hooked up with a group of Harvard contemporaries who published a law review dealing with labor law and farm problems. It was called the *IJA Review*, for International Juridical Association. They thought of it as a "radical" enterprise, and it was later listed as a Communist front organization. The chief organizer of the IJA was Shad Polier, who married Prossie's old friend Justine Wise and later became counsel to the American Jewish Congress. Lee Pressman was in the IJA as was another Harvard man, Nat Witt. Witt and Pressman worked in the Agricultural Adjustment Administration with Al, and Witt shocked Al in Washington by telling him that their work for the government was going to mean they would be earning big fees when they left the government for private practice. Witt and Pressman joined a Marxist study group in Washington, although Witt in the fifties wouldn't speak to

Pressman, who later became counsel to the CIO, because in 1950 Pressman testified that Witt and John Abt, another AAA lawyer, had been members of this group. Pressman also testified that Al had not been a member of this group. According to Chambers, the group was a Communist cell and Al and Donie were both in it. Donie, who didn't join any clubs, liked to play tennis and have people over for dinner. Al joined a non-Marxist study group in Washington — an informal monthly buffet supper club made up of an elite group of young experts who met to discuss foreign affairs. They were all State Department men, except Al, who was then in Justice; and included a Foreign Service officer, the head of the Latin American Division, and two economists, including the number two man in the economic adviser's office. Several members of this group were later accused of Communism. Noel Field, of the European Division, left the State Department in the late thirties to work for the League of Nations, which was considered quixotic and in bad taste — "You know, Noel, if you leave State, you can never come back to work here" — and helped repatriate East European Communists, many of whom became his friends, who had fought for the Loyalists in Spain. During the war he fed tidbits of information about the Germans from these guys to Allen Dulles, the head of OSS intelligence in Switzerland and Foster Dulles's brother.

After the war Noel Field disappeared in Hungary. It turned out he had been arrested by the Hungarian Communists as an imperialist spy. His wife came to look for him, and she disappeared. Eventually, they were both released from jail and given a house in Budapest. It has recently been revealed that Allen Dulles set Field up. He decided to scare the Communists by letting them know he had a vast American network in Eastern Europe, i.e., Field and his friends.

Larry Duggan, head of the Latin American Division and another member of the non-Marxist club, stayed in the State

Department. He was found dead on a ledge below an open office window in late 1948 while Nixon and the House Un-American Activities Committee were out after Al. Suicide? Accident? He'd just come back to town after a long flight. His body had one galosh on. The other galosh was in the room next to the window.

Chambers said that Al tried to recruit Charlie Yost, another member of the buffet club, to the Communist Party. Nixon, as President, made Yost ambassador to the United Nations. When reminded of Chambers' charges, Dick said, "Let bygones be bygones."

John Dickey, another member of this group, personal assistant to Francis B. Sayre, an old law professor of Al's and former son-in-law of Woodrow Wilson's, left State to practice law in Boston. Al was then hired by Sayre to take Dickey's place. Dickey was later president of Dartmouth and had his doubts about Al. He said Al had been in favor of making the veto part of the UN Charter and so had the Russians. Al said so had Senators Tom Connally and Arthur Vandenberg, the chairman and ranking Republican member of the Senate Foreign Relations Committee. "I'm very fond of John," Al tells me. "He's a nice guy." "Was Noel Field a dupe?" I asked Al the other day. "He was a Quaker," says Al. "What's that mean?" I said. "If he was a good guy, why didn't he take better care of himself?" "I think a lot of good people get crushed," Al says. "A lot of shits survive. And a lot of them get crushed, too." Al is sitting on his sofa with his feet up and a lap rug over his legs, smoking his pipe. I'm sitting on the other end of the sofa, and I've been asking him a lot of questions about the New Deal for weeks.

I never used to want to know about the New Deal, and Al's response has been New Deal 101a, a crash course in the subject. He's given me a dozen books and he's a good teacher because they're all interesting books — he doesn't force you to read the boring ones. He says he never wanted to push the subject on me, but now that I've asked . . . He's got his copy of the *Columbia Encyclopedia* on the floor next to him, so he can look up dates and people. But we find, on checking through the tome, that there are no entries for "Nye Committee," "Un-American," or "Martin Dies," father of the House Un-American Activities Committee. "Hiss, Alger," is in there, but "Chambers, Whittaker," isn't. "All the things I was interested in have disappeared," Al says. "Sunk without a trace. I don't know why the hell they have me in here."

Al's book on the New Deal is a very interesting document, quite unlike *In the Court of Public Opinion*, his book about the Hiss case, which a lot of people said had "no feeling." Al stopped working on the new book a couple of years ago when he saw Nixon starting to go down the drain because it seemed to him as if at last people might be ready to think Al had been framed and at last new evidence might come to light. The New Deal book has lots of feeling:

"I saw Roosevelt's victory as heralding a great national effort to eliminate the root causes of the social ills I had found so distressing — and which to my chagrin I was doing so little about. I was, therefore, already enlisted in spirit in the new administration and a partisan of its proclaimed reforms. Joining it was the fulfillment of strong but only partially conscious desires to give all my energies to some effective movement of reform. My mood was one of elation and I was confident that all over the country there were others like me who would join the ranks of the New Deal with the same feelings. As I arrived in Washington, I felt I had come to join a band of brothers. I was then twenty-eight, married and the step-father of a six-year-old son."

Al and Prossy lived in six different houses in Georgetown during the fourteen years they lived in Washington. Al always got to work before nine and usually stayed at the office until seven, eight, eight-thirty. He sometimes thought about how his work was keeping him away from Pros and Tim, but during the first three years in Washington he thought to himself, "I'm only down here for the duration of the emergency." During the next five years, from '36 through '41, he thought, "I'd better stick around because war is coming." Then, for four years after Pearl Harbor he thought, "I'll stay for the duration of the war." Finally, in 1946, it was, "I'm not going to resign under a cloud. I have to stay until my name is cleared." Al and Prossy had conventional sex together. Al and Prossy thought they never had any problems, Al says, except occasionally when Prossy was pissed. When Al got mad at Prossy he would take a walk around the block. Prossy played the piano, took premed courses for a while, dropped them, worked in the Library of Congress, was a civil defense warden in World War II, and eventually became a schoolteacher. People remember her as slim, pretty, with long hair, talkative, opinionated. Men rather liked her, women often found her a little scary.

Timmy was sent to progressive schools and didn't do very well. Al considered him "harum-scarum." In 1974 at his home in Eureka, California, Tim told Professor Allen Weinstein of Smith College, the man who says he has decided Al is guilty, that he had felt in the thirties that Al and Prossy weren't comfortable with each other in private, led no close personal life, and filled the time with "para-business things" — parties, dinners, shop talk over drinks. Tim felt that he didn't know either Al or Prossy very well, although they made a point of including him in activities. He was very lonely, he said, and the household remains something of a blur to him. "I assume they made love," he told the professor. "After all, Tony was born, but still that took a damned long time." Tim said he thought prison was the turning point of Al's life. "Before Hiss went into prison," Weinstein wrote in his notes,

"Hobson considers him — apparently — a severely repressed and morally-rigid figure, capable of inflicting all types of suffering upon himself in the name of his code of duty. He suggested that I get Hiss to discuss his relations with Frank Costello in prison (apparently Costello fascinated Hiss, who developed some sort of friendship or affinity toward the man). 'Prison changed him. He could never have left Priscilla before he went to prison, nor could he have sustained a relationship of the sort he has with Isabel before then.' He rambled at length on the effect of Alger upon Lewisburg and vice versa, using much of the material presented in Zeligs as illustration. (Zeligs is a psychiatrist who wrote a book saying Al's innocent.) He told one wonderful anecdote about his belief that prison had changed Hiss's character in fundamental ways. 'Until then, Alger had no sense of evil.' If Alger had been Hitler's jailer, Hobson said, he would have isolated him and made him extremely comfortable. Then, he would have begun an elaborate process of trying to reason with him politely about his views and actions, bringing him around if possible to a sense of decorum about life. (I HAVE RECONSTRUCTED THIS STORY BADLY. I'M CERTAIN IT IS ONE OF HOBSON'S FAVORITES AND I SHOULD ASK HIM TO REPEAT IT.)" Weinstein wasn't quite sure where Tim's information would fit into his own quest: "Although professing belief in his parents' complete innocence of Chambers' charges, Hobson provided some valuable information of mixed quality: some of which supported his arguments for innocence while other bits *might* help validate portions of Chambers' story."

Al's own memories of the thirties are of a wonderful time. "We young New Dealers" — this is from his unfinished book again — "were a select group. Our dedication and enthusiasm were heightened by the realization of our small numbers. There was work inside and outside the government for all of spirit and good intentions. Our mood was expansive and intolerant. Spring in Washington, that leisurely seasonal ceremony of blossoms and of intense greens throughout the city and the neighboring farmlands, was symbolic of our hopes and high spirits. We knew that we were caught up in one of the rare periods in history of rapid social change. Official responsibility in shaping that change was ours far beyond that of any group of young men since the days of the youthful Founding Fathers. We were a homogeneous lot, imbued from the outset with an esprit de corps. Our sense of community did not need to be stated. We assumed a solidarity and a spirit of comradeship; we took for granted a common set of values on which we tacitly based our daily actions. Our instinctive youthful loyalty to our peers was intensified by our common experience since the onset of the Depression. Shadings and subtleties of attitude, the usual bases for individualized feelings of separateness, had not been encouraged by the vast scale and catastrophic nature of the events we had become familiar with during the preceding three and a half years. In consequence, our shared opinions had a simplicity and clarity that enhanced the unity of outlook already made likely by our similar backgrounds.

"No more than a few thousand in number, we were disproportionately conspicuous. We stood out by reason of our youthful looks and manner, our formidable technical skills and brash self-confidence, our unbounded energy and zeal, our high morals and strong and shared sense of direction. We were marked, above all, by our gregariousness. We were inseparable. Circumstances formed us in small bands of roommates, associates in the same governmental agencies, and groups with similar interests like tennis or riding or square dancing or chamber music. But these were not self-centered or closed cliques, they were squads within the regiment of the young to which we gave our allegiance. As a body we flocked together spontaneously."

Al was almost not hired by the New Deal at all, he found out a couple of years ago when he ran into Lew Douglas in Tucson. Douglas was FDR's first budget director and subsequently president of Anaconda Copper. He told Al the story of signing a request by Henry Wallace, secretary of agriculture, for fifteen new men, including Jerome Frank, Al's immediate superior. The next day he got a request from Wallace for sixteen more men, including Al, and, being a cost-conscious man, refused his O.K. So Roosevelt called him up and said, "You should hear what Henry Wallace has been saying about you — you're sabotaging the New Deal." Douglas said, "Well, I'll approve them if you'll give me a copy of Wallace's memo!" Roosevelt said, "You're not even supposed to know about that, but O.K."

Al's first New Deal job, working for Jerry Frank, whose title was general counsel to the AAA, was a hot spot. Al became something of a hero in the job; he was almost fired once, threatened to quit on another occasion, and was resented by Frank and several others when he didn't quit on a third occasion. The AAA was a massive agency set up to do something right away to straighten out 50,000,000 farmers. The farmers had made a killing during World War I raising crops for the army and for the starving Europeans on 40,000,000 acres that had previously been grassland. They kept on producing throughout the twenties but didn't have those markets anymore. So by '33 cotton was selling for a nickel a bale and a ton of corn was going for $3.33.

Wallace and his deputy, Rex Tugwell, one of the Brain Trusters and considered the handsomest man in the New Deal, had two schemes: one was to give money to farmers directly and help put their incomes on a "parity" with factory workers; the other was to pay farmers by renting land from them or buying animals so they would cut back production. This caused a flap because the '33 crops were already in the ground, and it meant asking farmers to plow up every third row of cotton, for instance. There were stories about how mules that had been trained for years to avoid the crops refused to step on the plants, and a lot of sympathy was generated for the little pigs the government was slaughtering. But the AAA had remarkable success in signing up farmers to reduction contracts, and giant check-writing machines that impressed the hell out of visiting Russians — they were supplied to the government by a new firm called IBM; that's how old Tom Watson got his start — were sending cash out all over the country, and American farm income rose from $4 billion in 1932 to $6 billion in 1934.

One of Al's jobs as a lawyer was to help write the contracts, and he can still remember "feeling like a proconsul" — dashing a draft of a contract down to the government printing office in the middle of the night and then watching as a million copies of what he had just written came off the presses. "That's twice as many copies as *The New Yorker* sells every week," Al recalls.

Cotton was what made the job a hot seat, because cotton was the only crop that had once been raised by slaves and was in the thirties being raised by sharecroppers, the South's de-Reconstruction substitute for slavery. The men who had to sign up the big white cotton farmers to AAA contracts were county agents, local good ole boys whose salaries were paid partly by the Department of Agriculture and partly by various states. They tended to be good friends with the plantation owners. Roosevelt also had a theory that it was good politics and useful for his own peace of mind to put at the top of any department several people with very different ideas and followings. So in Agriculture, in addition to Tugwell, who had written a poem saying, "Let's roll up our sleeves and make America over," and Wallace, who played tennis in his socks, had good ideas, consulted a tea-leaf reader, and was

friends with Roerich, the mystic who founded the Tibetan
museum in New York and sent Department agricultural experts on expeditions to Mongolia, you had, on one hand,
Jerome Frank, Al's boss, a bright corporation lawyer from
the big cities who couldn't sleep except during the after-
noons in air-cooled movies and who chased after every girl
in the office, and on the other hand, George Peek, the first
administrator of AAA, Frank's boss, an old-time farm reformer interested only in parity. Peek, in the twenties, had
been president of the Moline Plow Company, a big outfit
that went smash and was liquidated by Jerome Frank as lawyer for one of the creditors. All Peek could see about the
Triple A, as he later wrote, was

> A plague of young lawyers settled on Washington. They all
> claimed to be friends of somebody or other and mostly of
> Felix Frankfurter and Jerome Frank. They floated airily into
> offices, took desks, asked for papers and found no end of
> things to be busy about.
>
> I never found out why they came, what they did or why
> they left.

Well, I don't want to belabor this, but the point is Al got
himself immediately right smack into the middle of a big
situation, and not everybody who joined the New Deal did.
Donie became a New Dealer lawyer after his year with
Holmes was over in '33, but he went into the Public Works
Administration, then to Interior, and then to Labor, where
things were less explosive. There were about a hundred young
New Dealer lawyers working for Frank, and Al was one of the
few who had ever seen a farm The typical joke about them
was that Lee Pressman, drawing up a code to regulate the
macaroni business, kept asking, "Will this code be fair to the
macaroni growers?" They all worked in a huge new building
Herbert Hoover had put up in the middle twenties at a time
when he was building huge new buildings for every depart-

ment all over Washington. Al was loyal to: the young lawyers; Frank; and Wallace, who he assumed was on Frank's side — even though Frank was paranoid and Wallace was goofy. Al disdained civil service tenure, was contemptuous of the political appointees Jim Farley sent over, and he went around the office saying, "Peek's no damn good." It was Al's opinion that there were two kinds of lawyers: one told his client what he couldn't do; the other, the New Dealer, told the client how to do, legally, what he wanted to do already. An old-timer, a civil service man Al liked, a lawyer, a career man in the Agriculture Department's solicitor's office who stayed on in Washington and eventually became Commissioner of Internal Revenue, told Al how to stay out of trouble. The two of them worked on some opinion together, and Al deferentially handed it to his friend for his official signature. "Uh-uh," said the guy. "You sign it. I've got a kid in school and a fifteen-thousand-dollar mortgage, and I've got to be here after you guys are gone. It's not that I don't believe in it. I'd sign it if it was the only way to get it through. But under the circumstances — you sign it." Al signed happily. "We didn't give a fuck," as he says.

Al started getting praise and blame. The P.R. man for the Triple A put out a press release about Al that got in the papers. Al had been out riding at a stable in Virginia with Timmy one Sunday — the country was only fifteen minutes from town in those days — and Tim's nag looked like it was getting away from him at one point. Al, keeping his eye on the "wild" eight-year-old, cantered up to grab Tim's bridle. Tim's saddle blanket suddenly fell off, Al's horse shied, and Al fell and cracked a couple of vertebrae. Then Al told the doctor, an All-American from Maine named Ledbetter: no cast, just a corset, steel or whalebone or whatever, because he had to get right back to work.

The press release called this "the Spirit of the New Deal."

And Bev Smith, an old Baltimore newspaper chum of Bosley's, put Al's picture — along with pictures of Jerome Frank and Abe Fortas — in a piece in the February 1934 *American Magazine* called "Uncle Sam Grows Younger." "Youth is in the saddle," Smith wrote about the New Dealers, but not necessarily referring to Al's accident, "riding hell-bent for victory or a fall. They have tremendous enthusiasm, and are working with a fury which threatens many of them with a nervous breakdown. As for Alger Hiss, why, the last time I remember seeing him he was roller skating with the other kids on Mosher Street in Baltimore. Now, in his twenties, he is one of the men chiefly responsible for the plan to buy $650,000,000 worth of commodities to feed the unemployed. He has too much spirit for his bodily strength and is in danger of working himself to death."

Al was also denounced to the FBI as a Red. One of the political appointees in Jerry Frank's office was a Mrs. Fuller, Jimmie Byrnes's sister, who didn't do much work, so the New Dealer lawyers were rude to her. She responded by sending a letter to J. Edgar Hoover denouncing them by name as Reds and quoting their anti-Peek remarks. Al found out about this because one of the young lawyers in the office, a chap named Morgan, left the agency to become an FBI agent and told him of seeing the report. Al thought it was funny. He had a run-in with Peek over some milk-marketing hearing in Boston. Lee Pressman was at the hearing for Frank's office and called up Al for a ruling on some matter. Al checked with Henry Wallace and called him back. Fifteen minutes later Peek called Al into his office and told him he was fired for disloyalty. "What have you been doing? Bugging my telephone?" asked Al. But it turned out Peek had sent a lawyer he had hired to the hearing, who had called him as soon as Lee Pressman had announced the anti-Peek ruling. Al explained that he had been acting under the directions of Henry Wallace, so that blew over.

The first major public split in New Deal ranks came in 1935 when Frank and Peek's successor, Chester Davis, another old pre–New Dealer farm reformer, fought each other to the death over the sharecroppers. The Davisites wanted to send AAA money for not planting cotton only to the big white cotton farm owners As one of the county agents explained it, "Imagine giving a check to a nigger cropper!" The Frankites wanted to send the sharecroppers' share directly to them. But the real issue was that the big farmers, with 40 percent of their land removed from cultivation under the terms of their Triple A contracts, wanted to get rid of 40 percent of their sharecroppers and cut down on overhead. Clause 7 of the 1934 cotton contract, which Al had helped draft, said that the big farmers had to keep the same number of sharecroppers on their farms. But it didn't say they had to keep the same actual *people.* So the farmers started getting rid of "troublemakers," i.e., sharecroppers who were trying to form a union, and replaced them with croppers who didn't give a shit. The Frankites thought that the Triple A had the power to force the farmers into line, simply by not paying them unless they behaved themselves. The Davisites thought this was A, silly, and B, would wreck the entire cotton economy.

Both sides, of course, assumed that Henry Wallace thought the way they did. But when push came to shove, Wallace went with Davis rather than lose most of his career professional staff and run into hot water with Congress, too. Frank, Pressman, and several other lawyers were let go, and the newspapers referred to the affair as a "purge." Shortly before the end, Al, thinking that Henry Wallace wanted to help the croppers, had helped write a legal opinion showing how Clause 7 could be interpreted to do that. Davis called him on the carpet and told him the opinion was "dishonest." Al was outraged and quit on the spot. But after a few minutes' conversation they figured each other out and Davis apologized and Al withdrew his resignation. So he was not one of the purgees. But by this time Al was already working full-time for the Nye Committee, though still on the AAA payroll, so he didn't quit when the others got fired, although he did go with Frank, at Frank's request, to see Wallace, where Frank demanded an explanation and learned only that Wallace had let Davis do the actual firing because he was afraid of facing Frank personally. Because he didn't quit, Frank thought Al was disloyal to him, and wouldn't testify for Al when Al got indicted thirteen years later.

My father was a decent, hardworking, blind fool in a pack of shrewd operators. Every time something needed to be done that the shrewd shuddered at, it was given to Al. So the Nixon case was the ultimate result of this. And Nixon has proved that sooner or later the shrewd are outshrewded.

It's hard to be good for long if you're not clever. It's hard to be clever for long if you're not good. Instead of getting respect, decent, hardworking government employees get used. That's the way Washington works. It's too bad.

The Nye Committee hearings about the munitions industry were held in the fall of '34 and the spring of '35. You don't hear too much these days about the Nye Committee, because the only result of the hearings was the Neutrality Act of 1935, which was a midthirties attempt to legislate the United States into having no foreign policy by mandating strict neutrality in any foreign dispute. This attitude was shortly superseded by World War II. The committee's backers were the American Legion, whose slogan was "Take the Profits Out of War," and the indefatigable Dorothy Detzer of the Women's International League for Peace and Freedom, who was out to get the "Merchants of Death." At the time the hearings got as much media attention as the Army-McCarthy Hearings or Sam Ervin's Watergate investigation. The secretary of the committee was Steve Raushenbush, who had gone after the coal industry and who was recommended for the job by Pat Jackson, an old Amherst buddy of Raushenbush's, an old pal of Al's sister Mary Ann, and later one of the AAA purgees who resented Al for not having quit. Al's job was counsel to the committee, which made him the Sam Dash of the Nye Committee, and his expectations of the hearings were (1) legislation to control international cartels dealing in armaments and (2) restrictive legislation to prevent profiteering in the case of war. Price and profit controls were in fact imposed during World War II and, as in the RCA case, nothing ever happened to the cartels. A midwestern paper wrote an editorial saying Al was aptly named for the job — Alger made you think of Horatio Alger, and Hiss represented the public's feelings toward the munitions industry. Halfway through the hearings Steve Raushenbush fell in love with an Irish girl, whose angle was that the U.S. had been sucked into World War I by J. P. Morgan and the British, and at that point the hearings changed course and headed toward the Neutrality Act of '35, and Al found a job in the Justice Department and said goomby.

Before that, armed with a subpoena, Al had spent weeks in Wilmington going over the books of the du Pont brothers, Irénée and Pierre, who tried to both bluster and cajole the young inquisitor. Irénée at one point said to Al, "Young man, don't forget you're our servant." Pierre then said soothingly, "He means you're a *public* servant." Later the du Ponts both offered him a job — "If you can't lick 'em, buy 'em," Al says — but he resisted their blandishments. Just think — Al today might be a retired du Pont V.P.! Al and the other committee lawyers also dug up a lot of facts about how the international munition firms — Skoda in Czechoslovakia, Bofors in

Sweden, Schneider-Creuzot in France, and Vickers and Imperial Chemical in England — had drummed up trade in the Chaco War of 1932–1935, a dispute between Paraguay and Bolivia in which a million lives were lost over a wasteland that was supposed to be sitting on oil. First the firms gave handouts to the sons and sons-in-law of various Latin American prime ministers, just the way the oil companies and the airplane companies do today, and the firms'd go to one country in the war and sell 'em a big order by telling them the other guys had just ordered the same stuff, which they hadn't yet — and then of course they'd go to the other guys . . .

Al grilled the du Ponts and the president of Curtiss-Wright Export at public committee sessions, and the senators also got him to ask all the tough questions when Bernard Baruch, who had been head of the War Industries Board under Wilson during World War I testified. Baruch was a South Carolinian who had made millions by the time he was thirty, who had advised Wilson, Harding, Coolidge, Hoover, and Roosevelt, and who was commonly rumored in the thirties to own sixty senators and representatives. Baruch was preceded on the stand by Jimmie Byrnes, then a senator from South Carolina, who gave Baruch a glowing character reference. Al then gave Baruch, who liked praise, a rough going over, which pissed Baruch to the extent that he afterward went around town calling Al a Red. And so again we see good blind Alger leaping in enthusiastically where angels fear to tread.

Al's exploits got into the papers in Washington and Baltimore and he was even mentioned once during the hearings in the *New York Times*. The reporters at the hearings were all over Al for information or copies of documents introduced into the record, but only one of them struck Al as in any way turned on by the importance of what he, Al, or the committee was doing for society. He can still remember clearly the words of Sir Wilmot Lewis, Washington correspondent for the London *Times*, who was not impressed: "Young man, you're wasting your time. These men rule our world, and they're not going to let you stop them."

So who was the one guy who told Al he thoroughly understood the work Al was doing and that he was doing a great job of work? Yes, it was the famous fat guy with the bad teeth, who told Al his name was George Crosley, a writer who had zero bucks but who was going to do a whole series of pieces on the Nye Committee for *American Magazine*. Enter Whit Chambers, "Beadle" to his dad, "Vivian" to his mom, "Stinky" in high school, "Carl" to Julian Wadleigh, a State Department officer who later gave him State Department papers, "Lloyd Cantwell" to his landlord in Baltimore, "David Breen" to the Passport Office, a.k.a. Jay Vivian Chambers (on his birth certificate), Charles Adams (for his grandpa Charles Whittaker and John Quincy Adams), Charles Whittaker, Jay Chambers (his dad's name), Whittaker Chambers, J. W. Chambers, David Chambers, David Whittaker Chambers, Jay V. David Chambers, David Zabladowsky, Jay David Chambers, Jay David Whittaker Chambers, John Kelly, John Land, George Cantwell, J. Dwyer, Vivian Dwyer, David Dwyer, David Whittaker Dwyer, the first man ever to translate *Bambi* into English, a man who in the thirties went around Greenwich Village telling everyone he was planning on becoming "the American Lenin." The dude who liked to go through people's wastebaskets and keep dossiers on people, who as a writer for *Time* set up secret assignations just to turn in stories, the Columbia classmate of art historian Meyer Shapiro's and of Lionel Trilling's, who once said the rottenness of Chambers' teeth persuaded him of the man's moral integrity.

Al was later, at indictment time, able to find only one person who had known "George Crosley" — Sam Roth, a New York book publisher — and Al's lawyers wouldn't let Roth testify at the perjury trials because Roth had done time for a porno conviction. Roth was quite pissed about this decision.

Chambers and Al started lunching occasionally — Dutch treat — at a beanery near Capitol Hill, and Chambers, in addition to telling Al what important work he, Al, was doing and actually receiving from him, Al, Nye Committee copies of genuine State Department documents — the committee had piles of them lying around to give to the press — talked literature and kept mentioning how hard up he was — the wife, the little girl to support. He mentioned he'd spent a summer as a migrant farm laborer out west, something Bosley had once done. He didn't talk Communism. (While we're at it, what *was* Al's attitude toward Communists at the time? A, Al didn't know any, or at least didn't know anyone who ever claimed to be a Commie. B, it wasn't illegal to belong to the Party. C, it was a free country. D, he hadn't ever read *Das Kapital* (he still hasn't). E, the New Deal was all in favor of sharecroppers and factory workers getting organized, and as far as he could see, a lot of the guys out in the heartland actually trying to do that, actually trying to implement government policy, and getting knocked on the head for it, were Communists. F, he never met her, but the word was that the best-dressed and most sophisticated reporter in Washington was the girl from the *Daily Worker*, and everyone who met her wanted to make it with her.

Al told Chambers he could sublet a partially furnished apartment he and Prossy had just moved out of but still had a three months' lease on. The apartment stayed available to Chambers even after he turned up on Al's doorstep with his wife and year-and-a-half-old daughter to spend a few days because his "furniture van hadn't arrived" and later when he failed to pay any rent of any kind, except on one occasion when he again appeared on the Hiss doorstep with the famous Persian rug — a rug that's now over at my place; it's folded up and serving as a cushion about a foot from my desk. A nice rug, a Tekke, red, white, black, and orange, unraveled a bit at one end — when I was in college I used to say Chambers had taken a bite out of it.

Al gave Chambers a "sassy" dark blue '29 Ford roadster worth about twenty-five dollars. He'd bought it in 1929 as a family car, but it turned out to be too small for his family. Al once drove Chambers to New York in his new car — a dealer's model '35 Plymouth — and happened to point out 1427 Linden Avenue on the way through Baltimore. He also periodically loaned Chambers five or ten dollars, loans which didn't stop just because Chambers never paid back. The only thing Al didn't do for Chambers was read aloud to him.

Al was, in fact, "intrigued" by Chambers, as he recalls. Why? Well, I hate to have to tell you this, because I personally find it a bit creepy, but the real reason, as Al admitted to me the other day, over and above Chambers' laying on the flattery about Al's job and his well-liked Renaissance Man conception, was that Al felt sympathy for Chambers. "I like people when they're in trouble," Al said. "Because then they have to like you, and you can feel powerful by helping them. I *love* to visit people in the hospital." And there you have it.

Whittaker Chambers leaves our story here. The thing Al remembered most clearly thirteen years later was the teeth. After a couple of years of knowing that character, Al finally decided that what he had on his hands was a "welsher," so when Chambers phoned him at the office one day he told him, over the phone, not in person, that he didn't think Chambers ever intended to pay back the money and that it was time "to cut the thing off."

Al's next job was in the solicitor general's office — he's the man who handles legal appeals to the Supreme Court for the United States government and argues them there — the government's chief barrister, the English would call him. He and his assistants always wore — still do wear — a morning coat and striped pants when appearing before the Court. They're the only people left in the country who wear cutaways to work. Al's first big job was writing the brief to defend the AAA, which was being attacked as unconstitutional. Al's boss, the solicitor general at the time, was Stanley Reed, a genial pol from Kentucky some ten years Al's senior, whose assistants liked him fine and thought perhaps his best quality as a lawyer was that he let bright men do their work unhindered. Al, or rather the government, lost the AAA case, 6-3, but Al won the one case he ever personally argued before the Supreme Court, *U.S.* v. *Knott,* and he enjoys saying that Dick Nixon lost the one case he ever personally argued before the Supreme Court. The two senior justices, who traditionally sit on either side of the chief justice, played a little cat and mouse with Al during the case — this is traditional with a young lawyer arguing before the Court for the first time. Al did all right. Judge Sutherland said, "Speak up, young man, don't mumble!" A couple of minutes later Judge McReynolds said, "You don't have to shout!" Al kept cool.

Al was delighted to be able to work on the AAA case because it fit right in with a secret about lawyering that he had discovered he thought for the first time, namely: the best way to approach a corporate case was to think of yourself, at least for a while, as actually working for your client's company, participating in its day-to-day activities. Of the old crack about lawyers, "The law sharpens your mind by narrowing it," Al says, "Well, you have to accept a slice, but the more I know about the pie, the better I can do. In the Gillette case I went out to the factory, in the RCA case I studied radio and vacuum tubes back to Marconi, and I thought I proved my theory on the Hoosack-Mills case, as the AAA case was known. A court will take what it calls 'judicial notice' of the established facts in any case, meaning the things that are uncontested.

Usually this doesn't amount to much, but the procedure had recently been extended to cover official publications. One of the sleights-of-hand we pulled in the case involved my going over to a couple of guys at the Triple A and having them write an official history of the agency. And I helped 'em write it. And of course it showed the agency in a sympathetic light. An ordinary lawyer, coming in from the outside, wouldn't have known that this was feasible. Every area of thought develops its own procedure. I would be superb if I ever had to handle a case for S. Novick," — S. Novick is the printing firm Al's been working for for the last sixteen years — "'cause I know all about production there, accounting, sales. I'd know who to call on as they became relevant. The average lawyer in the thirties used to look down on this house-counsel kind of approach to the law, but the fellow who's now president of Anaconda Copper used to work in my friend Robbie Von Mehren's law office handling the Anaconda account, so of course he got to know every nook and cranny, every in and out of the company. Which means that my discovery has now become a fact of the business forty years later.

"The other thing I liked about my approach to the law — what I liked about the law was its accuracy, succinctness, orderliness, completeness — what I liked about my approach was totally immersing yourself in a case — was that it meant you had all the excitement of being a student again for a while, and then you went on to something else. When I was finished with the AAA case, then I was all ready to go to the State Department. We used to think that a lawyer with a specialty, a man like John Mitchell, who specialized in bonds, was a dull plod who might as well be working in a bank. I did some work on trade agreements in the SG's office — part of the New Deal approach to foreign policy was freer trade and lower tariffs negotiated through a system of reciprocal trade agreements with different countries — and when Francis

Sayre — Francis B. Sayre, Assistant Secretary of State for Economic Affairs and former son-in-law of Woodrow Wilson — suggested I come over to State and work on trade agreements from within the department, this fit right in with my theory and I became house counsel, in effect, to the State Department on trade agreements. After that, I was Mr. Trade Agreements on legal questions. If an assistant attorney general wanted a conference on trade agreements, I was the guy who knew the subject."

At Justice, Al worked in another big, new Hoover-built pile, more grandiose than the new Agriculture Building. He was one of Stanley Reed's two chief assistants — the other was Paul Freund, the constitutional law scholar at Harvard whom Kennedy wouldn't appoint to Frankfurter's seat on the Supreme Court because he had refused to serve first as Kennedy's solicitor general. Freund's big case, while Al was working on the Triple A appeal, was defending the constitutionality of the TVA, successfully, as it turned out. Down the hall from Stanley, Paul, and Al were the offices of the attorney general and of J. Edgar Hoover. When Al was with Stanley Reed he occasionally rode up or down with Hoover in the SG's, AG's, and FBI director's private elevator. But they did not pass the time of day together.

The New Dealers in the SG's office considered Hoover a time-server, a publicity hound, and an upstart. Stanley Reed himself knew nothing whatever about Hoover's activities. When Al introduced Reed to George Biddle, brother of Attorney General Francis Biddle, who had been hired by the WPA to paint some murals in the Justice Department, neither man knew what to say to the other, so Biddle said, "I see you've caught Alvin Karpis" — the name just under Dillinger's on the FBI's Ten Most Wanted list. Reed mumbled something, and when Biddle took off Reed asked Al, "Was he talking about 'Parkyakarkis'?" — a popular radio comedian who did an act as a Greek.

Stanley Reed, who was appointed to the Supreme Court in 1938, was later a character witness for Al in his trials and two years ago sent in an affidavit to the Massachusetts Bar Association supporting Al's application for readmission. Felix Frankfurter was also a character witness at the trials — one reason why Al went to jail. Since Reed and Frankfurter had testified, they had to disqualify themselves from voting on whether to take the case when Al appealed it to the Supreme Court. The newest justice at the time, Tom Clark, also disqualified himself because he had been attorney general at the time the indictments were being prepared. This left six judges, a bare quorum, and only two, William Douglas and Hugo Black, voted to take the case. Reed and Frankfurter would have voted to take the case and four out of eight or nine is always enough for a hearing. According to Douglas in his autobiography, *Go East, Young Man*, the court would have had to throw out the Hiss case because in 1945 they had decided unanimously that in perjury cases you have to have either two witnesses or one witness and "trustworthy evidence."

Douglas and Abe Fortas, who had been Douglas' best student at Yale, had tried to hire Al to work for the SEC in '34 to investigate how reorganization committees swindled companies that had gone into bankruptcy and receivership. Douglas and Fortas had heard Al was an "outstanding" lawyer in the AAA, so they took him out to dinner at the Carlton Hotel, but Al turned them down flat. "That was the first and last I ever saw of the man," Douglas wrote. "But as troubled days came upon him, I wondered whether fate would have served him differently if he had chosen Wall Street and predatory finance as his specialty rather than agriculture and, later, foreign affairs. As to the Hiss case," said Douglas, "the perjury rules adopted by the Supreme Court say evidence, if you have only one witness, must establish 'independent proof of facts inconsistent with the innocence of the accused.' This rule was adopted both because the Court recognized the weakness of memory as a tool and because it saw a need to protect 'honest witnesses from hasty and spiteful retaliation in the form of unfounded perjury prosecutions.' Probably the evidence most damaging to Hiss was the fact that some of the incriminating documents were typed on a typewriter once owned by Hiss. There was no evidence that Hiss or Mrs. Hiss did the typing. The typing might have been done by Chambers or by any stooge of Chambers'. It was not even certain that at the relevant times the old typewriter was even owned by Hiss or was under his control. Moreover, on a later motion for a new trial, there was offer of proof that the typewriter — the one said to belong to Hiss — was itself a 'forgery,' manufactured to have all the characteristics of the old Hiss typewriter.

"Certain it is that the inference that Hiss was 'framed' was strong. The case illustrates the wisdom of having two witnesses on a perjury charge or if there is only one, as in the Hiss case, that the court ride herd on the nature of the corroborative evidence, to make certain it has that 'trustworthy' character which will prevent one accused of perjury from being 'framed.'

"In my view no court at any time could possibly have sustained the conviction."

Al had one other disastrous day in court while working for Stanley Reed, but it was hardly his fault. One of the pieces of legislation being attacked as unconstitutional was a non–New Deal bill called the Bankhead Act, sponsored by the senior senator from Alabama, Tallulah's uncle, that set up rigidly enforced quotas for the big cotton growers. Al and his pals thought the act was clearly unconstitutional on the face of it, and not only that but "Prussian" and "totalitarian," and since Al's hero at the time was former Solicitor General and Attorney General William D. Mitchell, a courtly man who had been known in his day as "the tenth man on the Supreme Court" and one who had routinely refused to appeal cases he thought had no basis in law, Al urged Stanley Reed to drop the case. But Stanley didn't want to be identified as the man who had made that decision and thought it should be left to the Court to strike down the act. So Al had to prepare some arguments Stanley Reed could use to defend the thing, but when Reed got on his feet before the Court, all the judges gave him such a hard time that he realized he had nothing to say, so he fainted and had to be carried out of the Court. Al, who was with him, had to finish arguing the case for the government.

Charlie Horsky's strongest recollection of Al at that time is the night he came into the office between 2:00 and 3:00 A.M., found Al hard at work and another guy they both knew, a Triple A lawyer, conked out on a table. "What's he doing here?" Charlie asked. "Oh," said Al, "I thought I might need to ask him a couple of questions, so I asked him to stay."

And now for something completely different: the United States Department of State. In the thirties in Washington they said, "The writ of the New Deal runs everywhere — except the State Department." According to Al, it was a very jolly place to be. According to Charlie Darlington, one of Al's pals in the department, who in the sixties was named ambassador to Gabon by Lyndon Johnson, "It was a club. It was a nice small place full of the right sort, although I suppose I'm a snob to say that. There were a couple of hundred officers in the department. Documents were always signed at the bottom with the initials of the office and the writer, and you always knew who the writer was. Now there are so many different departments you have to look in a book just to see what the department is." Most of the officers were career Foreign Service men who either didn't need or didn't want political bases in Congress for support — which also meant that when they came under attack in the forties they didn't have any political bases in Congress to support them. They worked in an old building across the street from the White House that, unlike Herbert Hoover's structures, had been built to take the Washington heat. The place had black and white marble floors, tall ceilings, louvered doors, and green and white striped awnings over the south and west windows in the summer. Al said the building looked like a Mississippi River steamboat and that "the State Department taught you always to hew to the middle of the road because if you didn't, the louvered doors could swing out and swat you."

Security? "I suppose we locked the door at night," says Charlie Darlington, who at the time was one of the assistant chiefs of the Trade Agreement Division. "Papers we left on desks or in a drawer. Anyone could come in — I often found Julian Wadleigh at my desk when I came back from lunch going through papers. I wasn't even annoyed. In the sixties when I was ambassador to Gabon — by then everything was a secret. The department sent over position papers, background material on the country. I put 'em in my briefcase to read at home at night — only hours I had free to look at 'em. My security man was shocked. 'Mr. Ambassador, those papers must not leave the building.' 'Well, how'm I ever going to read them, then?' 'Sir, I don't know.' So I never read them. I went to Rio Muni — hardly anyone had been there at that point, very remote, spent three days with the then Spanish governor of that little enclave in his palace. Sent off a report to the department — it was mostly travelogue, although I'd had a very interesting time. My security man was shocked again. 'You didn't mark it "SECRET" or "CLASSIFIED," Mr. Ambassador.' 'Well, it isn't.' 'Sir, everything we send out is either secret or classified.' So I let him rush off a cable to mark my report classified on arrival. He felt much better."

There was some sort of security apparatus in the State Department in Al's day. He remembered a little guy named Murphy who used to run around and say things like, "I'm worried about Sumner Welles." And I've got a copy of Al's State Department security file here which starts off, "NAME: HISS, ALGERNON." There were a lot of very bright and, for Washington, unusual guys in the State Department. Fellows like Adolf Berle, whom Dean Acheson called "the boy wonder." He had graduated from Harvard at the age of eighteen and he and his wife, who was a doctor, had two bathtubs in the bathroom so they could take baths together without interrupting their conversations. There was a White Russian named Leo Pasvolsky who wrote most of the United Nations charter, collaborating in the final stages with a Soviet diplomat, a Red Russian named Sobolev. Leo, who was a good friend of Al's, was known as "the brain that walked like a man." Al's two closest buddies in the Department wanted, respectively, more trade with the Nazis and more trade with the Japs.

The only unclubbable man in the State Department was Julian Wadleigh, an economist who didn't brush his hair or his shoes, whom Chambers, under the moniker "Carl," persuaded to give him State Department papers. Wadleigh did this instead of writing a novel, according to Mike Zeligs' *Friendship and Fratricide: An Analysis of Whittaker Chambers and Alger Hiss*. "I was enormously impressed with Chambers' fund of knowledge of events," Wadleigh told Zeligs. "I could scarcely mention a country in the world but Carl would speak with an intimate knowledge of it. I wanted to get out of the cloisters and into the world, so I had to work with the Communists. I guess I should have been in a university. I liked Whit, I really did! My grievance is against the world, for they know me only because of the piddling things I did for the Communist Party." Wadleigh considered Al a very moderate New Dealer with strongly conservative instincts and was shocked and confused when Chambers fingered Al. Of course, there's no evidence to show that the papers Wadleigh gave Chambers ever went anywhere near the Communist Party. All we know is some of them turned up empumpkined thirteen years later in the middle of the night on Whit's farm in Westminster, which was, by the way, a piece of land that Al had contemplated buying at the time he knew "George Crosley." But the owner died and, it looked like the price was going to go up, so Al got his $500 deposit back and Chambers scampered off and secured possession of the dump.

Al's first boss at State, Frank Sayre, was a quiet, restrained, formal, very religious high church Episcopalian who liked to go on retreats and who in profile closely resembled his famous former father-in-law, Woodrow. Al sometimes suspected that he sat so that light would catch his profile. Al liked him. Al also always had very good relations with Mrs. Shipley, another higher-up, and old battle-axe who ran the passport office in the State Department. Al knew how to wheedle Mrs. Shipley into processing passport applications for friends quickly. Everyone else tried to pull rank on her, which was a mistake, as she would then coldly ask them: "Is this request official? Will this help the foreign policy of the United States?" They would get embarrassed and retreat in confusion. Al would call up and say, "I know you're overburdened, and I'm not asking a favor," and Mrs. Shipley would say, "Look, we have so many applications, it doesn't matter which we take up first. Put Mr. Hiss's friend on top of the pile."

Al says he worked this trick eight or ten times over the course of ten years. "Mrs. Shipley had perfect control of Congress — as good as J. Edgar's — because she did favors for all the congressmen. She kept Paul Robeson from getting a passport, and one time during the war she came to me in a state of agitation and said, 'Mr. Hiss, Eleanor Roosevelt wants to send some pacifists to Chungking,' — the American Friends Service Committee wanted to send an ambulance to the Chinese wartime capital — 'we're trying to get the Chinese to *fight!* Can't you do anything about it?' I liked her. She was a very spicy, self-possessed, intelligent little lady." Mr. Sayre's brother, a radical Episcopal priest, the Reverend John Nevin Sayre, for whom Whittaker Chambers' wife, Esther, once worked as a secretary, was unable to get a passport. Mrs. Shipley explained that the brother was a bad risk. Sayre, infuriated, got hold of his brother's FBI file. This was the first FBI file Al had ever seen. The charges in it were that John Sayre was a member of the Fellowship of Reconciliation, a pacifist, and that he read *The Nation.* Sayre hit the roof and his brother got the passport.

In 1959 Al had trouble getting a passport. This was after Mrs. Shipley's time. I was graduating high school and going to go off to Europe for the first time with some friends and Al figured maybe he'd come along too and anyway he'd like to have a passport. This was when he was four years out of jail and it was a couple of months after he left mom. The State Department held up Al's passport for months because the FBI told them someone had told them Al's real purpose in making the trip, which he never made, was to meet a Soviet courier in East Berlin.

Sayre's assistant secretaryship for economic affairs included, for some reason, overseeing the Philippines, then still a dependency of the U.S., and one of his accomplishments was drafting the Philippine Independence Act. Al, who sat in the outer office, got to meet Manuel Quezon, the Philippine president, and discovered, he said, for the first time just how good first-class Philippine cigars are. Al asked Quezon whether he'd ever met Dean Fansler, Prossy's brother, and Quezon said, "He was my teacher," and showed Al a debating medal he always carried with him that Dean had presented him. Sayre liked to take Al to lunch at Herzog's, an expensive seafood joint near the Mayflower Hotel four blocks from the State Department frequented by pols and lobbyists, which Al couldn't afford. Sayre always offered to pay, Al always insisted on going Dutch, Sayre always had both chocolate and vanilla ice cream, Al always found this evidence of essential simplicity. They lunched there the day the Munich Pact was signed. Sayre said: "This is either one of the darkest days in history or a red letter day." Al said: "I think it's a terrible sellout." Sayre said: "I hope you're wrong, Alger." Al wrote speeches for his boss, but this was mostly cut-and-paste, once Al discovered the speeches Sayre liked best were the ones he'd already made.

Al has some good State Department stories, most of which I've just heard for the first time. He used to like to talk more about policy, but I guess he doesn't mind telling the stories now that I've convinced him I'll never be high-minded. Like the one about King ibn-Saud of Arabia to whom the Americans, during the war, gave a walkie-talkie as a present. He didn't know what it was for, so an officer explained that the King could command a jeep to drive out of sight behind a sand dune and could then, simply by talking into the dingus, make it reappear. Saud was delighted and spent the rest of the afternoon making a jeep vanish and return.

As Sayre's assistant Al once met Douglas MacArthur, who came to pay a courtesy call after retiring as chairman of the Joint Chiefs of Staff. Sayre, who didn't like him, told Al after MacArthur left: "He's in a box. He's very restless and uncertain, but it's a tradition that once you've been chairman of the Joint Chiefs you can't accept any lesser post." MacArthur, however, did. Quezon made him marshall of the Philippines, meaning head of the local militia, and paid him seventy-five grand a year for doing nothing. The guys in the State Department considered this *"infra-dig"* among themselves. Later, on Pearl Harbor Day, they called MacArthur a "dumdum" but for morale purposes never announced the story of the general's actions in the hours after Pearl. MacArthur's regular army commission had been reactivated some months before the Japanese attack. Right after the attack he took all his fighter planes into the air and cabled the War Department for permission to attack Japanese planes on Formosa.

Al was at home Pearl Harbor Sunday listening to the Philharmonic on the radio after lunch when the broadcast was interrupted for news of the attack. "I did a double take. My first reaction was, 'Did you hear what I heard?' Then I dashed down to the office. Pandemonium. Everybody else had dashed down, too, none of us quite knowing what the hell to do. We didn't even know whether we were at war, because the Japanese hadn't yet declared it, and their ambassadors were still in Washington. Was this just the independent action of one Japanese admiral? Was it an act of war? We spent all afternoon running in and out of each other's offices and making calls back and forth. The only hard news we had was a cable that had come in the day before, in the late afternoon, saying that a strong Japanese fleet had been seen sailing off the coast of Indochina toward Khota Bharu, but that there was a strong possibility that this was only a feint. I had never heard of Khota Bharu, nobody had ever heard of Khota Bharu. And after all, that threat, if it existed, seemed to be only against the British in Malaya or the Dutch in the East Indies. When MacArthur's cable arrived people yelled, 'Why the hell is he asking? Why the hell doesn't he do anything? Why doesn't he act *without* authority?' Since we didn't know if war was on, we couldn't officially authorize anything, but if he had acted on his own initiative, and it turned out there was no war, even if he had to be court-martialed no one would have taken that seriously. MacArthur, however, not getting an answer back from us, brought his planes down for lunch. While he was eating, they were all wiped out on the ground, wing to wing, by Japanese bombers, seven hours after Pearl Harbor.

"Well, we couldn't say, at the outset of the war, that the senior American general in the area had lost all his planes because of his own inaction. General Short and Admiral Kimmel, the commandants at Pearl, were court-martialed, but not MacArthur. Much later the Far Eastern Division of the State Department, where I was working at the time of Pearl, got flak from crank reactionaries who said we'd set up Pearl, provoked it, by ignoring Japanese attempts to negotiate. These days some revisionist historians are promoting the same line, but the facts are, the only deal the Japanese ambassadors were offering was: the U.S. could trade with and invest in Japan *if* we stopped supporting China and gave the Japanese domination of Malaya and the Dutch East Indies. If, that is to say, we ceded the Far East to the Japanese and their Greater East Asia Co-Prosperity Sphere."

A year before Pearl, Frank Sayre was made high commissioner to the Philippines, and Al got the job of being personal assistant to Stanley Hornbeck, political adviser on Far Eastern Affairs, a career man in his sixties who had been chief of the division, and then promoted in a management/ efficiency move that relieved all the division chiefs of administrative duties in order to "free them for thinking." It was the general opinion in the department that Stanley was a bear — his secretaries routinely applied for transfers after a year for reasons of health, meaning, invariably, that they were getting fat. Every time Stanley got mad he yelled at his secretary, and every time he yelled at his secretary he gave her a box of candy the next day. A secretary of Stanley's accumulated a lot of candy in the course of a year.

Stanley Hornbeck, five-nine or -ten, in his early sixties, with a few gray wisps of hair carefully combed back over his cranium, a man who could be heard in the halls whenever he yelled, was an Anglophile from Colorado and one of the first Rhodes scholars. He taught in China as a young man, although he never learned Chinese, and early on decided that Japan was a menace. He was scholarly, thorough, informal with Al; crusty, tense, demanding, and exacting with most of his colleagues; courtly and courteous to his wife, a widow and former Sweetbriar administrator whom he had married late and who cooed at his attentions. The Hornbecks lived in a spartan, slightly run-down apartment on Wyoming Avenue. Al thought Stanley flattered his wife and spoiled her. Stanley thought of himself as sort of the permanent undersecretary of state — in England the civil servant who minds the store and watches the political appointees come and go. Stanley never yelled at Al. He was Al's favorite boss — except, I guess, Sam Chernoble, the guy who hired him as a printing salesman in 1959 at a point when no one else seemed to want to put him to work.

"Alger," Stanley asked, after they were good friends, "why do you think I'm here in this office? It isn't money — you know what we all get paid. It's power. I can have greater power, greater influence on events than I could anywhere else. I'm just a guy from Colorado."

Al liked this kind of talk. "I was glad," he says, "to be working for a man who knew his objectives, who was so clear-eyed about them, and I felt I could share in his objectives. At no time while I was in the State Department did I feel I was doing menial work, chores. A stream of fascinating people passed through Mr. Hornbeck's office, and I chatted with them while they were waiting to see him. He had excellent relations with the military — General Embick, a member of the Joint Chiefs, came over a lot, and General George Strong, the chief of G–2, as army intelligence was called at the time, and General Fairchild of the Air Force, a very broad-gauge, wise, cultivated man, charming, who died young, and Stilwell, and Colonel Evans Carlson — he was one of the most extraordinary. A soft-spoken, lanky, hardworking fieldman (not a brass hat) he was too outspoken ever to be made a general. His father had been a pastor in Peacham, the tiny town in northeastern Vermont Prossy and I started taking summer vacations in during the thirties, and he had been the parson's bad boy — sliding downhill in the winter on the snow on barrel tops. He had been out in China as military attaché for a while, and he believed in the reality of the Chinese Communist military power from the start — he saw that as the only organized, efficient, uncorrupt force in the country they had to win, sooner or later. During World War II he headed Carlson's Raiders, a famous fighting group in the Pacific that went island hopping with great dash and success. Jimmy Roosevelt was in that group."

"Did you know Jimmy Roosevelt?"

"Yeah, sure, when he was courting Betsy Cushing, remember? He was attractive, charming, rather weak, a soft personality, not assertive or strong. He was a Harvard Law dropout and a BU grad. Went into the insurance business."

Hornbeck's office faced the White House. Al was still working in this room, though by then functioning as part of the division planning for the UN, the day FDR died. In fact, he was the first person in the State Department to hear about it. He got a call from Jack Peurifoy, an advance man in San Francisco making arrangements for the United Nations Organizing Conference. "Jack said, 'We've just had a report the President's dead.' I said, 'That can't possibly be true. Hold the line.' I called McDermott, the department press man, and asked him if he'd heard anything. He said, 'No.' Then I said, 'Hey, wait a minute. There are a lot of people running toward the White House.' It was the press people, who'd just heard, running like crazy. I went into a real state of funk. The whole State Department went into a real state of funk. I went out and walked the streets. I saw tears, people filing into churches. I can't remember if I called Prossy. As I would have wanted to. Or should have done."

5. Everything I Always Wanted to Know about Alger Hiss but Was Afraid to Ask

IN THE SPRING of 1944, a year before Roosevelt died, when Al was thirty-nine, he was drafted by the State Department into a new division called the Office of Special Political Affairs, which was planning for the United Nations. His old boss, Stanley Hornbeck, was leaving the department: Hornbeck was shortly thereafter named ambassador to the Netherlands. For the previous two years, Al had been sitting in on postwar planning as Hornbeck's deputy. Postwar planning began in the State Department shortly before the United States entered World War II. Leo Pasvolsky, the man behind the United Nations Organization — you will remember that he was "the brain who walked like a man" — had been working since then on a plan for some kind of international postwar cooperative organization. As Hornbeck's deputy on the Committee on Post-war Planning, Al had spent many hours discussing among other things the fate of the Emperor of Japan. "People like Stanley and me — we were usually in agreement," Al says, "thought that as long as the Emperor was there, the old martial spirit of Japan wouldn't be broken. Reischauer and a couple of others took the other position.

They said we didn't realize what chaos would ensue in Japan if the Emperor was deposed. We thought the Japanese should be not only humbled but restructured democratically. It was really an argument between the Japanese experts in the department, who agreed with Reischauer, and the China experts. Finally, a compromise was reached. We kept the Emperor but he became our puppet and MacArthur became the Mikado of Japan after the war. I'm inclined to think the Japan experts were right. Certainly having the Emperor there made occupation a lot easier for us. We didn't need a large occupying force speaking Japanese. A couple of years ago I saw films, on that BBC series, 'The World at War,' of weeping Japanese who would have otherwise fought to the death surrendering because their Emperor had told them to surrender."

Al's new job in '44 working with Pasvolsky led him within a year to the Yalta Conference, a.k.a. the Crimea Conference, on the shore of the Black Sea in Russia, a summit conference between Roosevelt, Stalin, Churchill, and their aides, and, a few months after that, to the San Francisco Organizing Conference of the United Nations. At Yalta, Al was a technical adviser to the American delegation, and in San Francisco, he was Secretary-General of the Conference. Or as he puts it, chief cook and bottle washer. Butler and silver polisher might be even closer to it. Like most of Al's New Deal assignments, these two conferences later turned out to be highly controversial, and, in retrospect, one can see once again that Al had jumped into a couple of hot spots. The Yalta Conference was, during the later forties and early fifties, denounced up and down and over and under and left and right, as the sellout of American interests to the Russians, and people like the John Birchers who don't like the UN, which they still call The House That Hiss Built.

The other day I asked Al how come he landed in so many

hot spots. He said, "Well, they were all points of action. I never had a dull assignment in Washington, and, after all, I went down to Washington in order to be useful." He sees it as a matter of course. As for the job working under Pasvolsky, he went on, "I was a pretty logical choice of the younger people who could be detached for special service. When you get an assignment like that in the State Department, it seems logical. It's like the player draft in baseball. If you don't want to be a free agent, you just automatically take the job. And I was pleased. I would have had the sort of automatic approval of Hull, who was still nominally secretary of state even though he was sick, or of Dean Acheson. They would have said, 'Fine — good choice,' if anyone had asked them.

"As far as I know I had no competition for the job. There was Harley Notter, who'd been working for Pasvolsky, who was a little put out when I got the job. I guess in one sense, I came in from — well, I won't say left field because Weinstein would catch us up on that. Harley mumbled about it and he was one of the few people in the department who didn't spring to my defense when Chambers' charges came up. I think Leo Pasvolsky told me later — now that I think about it, *he* was one of the people who picked me. He wanted someone with departmental contacts. And he didn't want to do any administrative work himself. I worked with Leo without any hitches."

Al's new hot spot was just about as complicated as the Triple A situation in the thirties. FDR believed in some form of postwar international organization and so did his new secretary of state, Ed Stettinius. So the ideas of Pasvolsky and his boys were taken seriously in the department as long as those two guys were on the scene. But there was a large section of the State Department, the European Division, which was led by a man named Jimmy Dunn, that saw Leo as a temporary aberration. Al's friend former Brandeis clerk

Dean Acheson, for instance, a European Division ally, never believed in the UN but was too polite to say so until the day after his death in the 1970s — he confided his sentiments beforehand only to Alden Whitman, then the crack obit writer for the *New York Times.*

Al on the subject of the European Division: "I've heard it said that the State Department are the vestal virgins of American foreign policy, keeping a sacred fire going. I heard one of the European Division guys say once, 'Roosevelt? He's only been elected President four times.' These people tended to think of Presidents as hacks and, of course, Presidents often were. Presidents came and went but they were always there to uphold American interests." The European Division also tended to think of Russia as America's principal enemy, or rival, or the bad guys, or the team to beat. There were also plenty of other people who felt that way in other departments. Allen Dulles, Foster's brother, who ran the OSS Office, the wartime intelligence office, in Berne, Switzerland, spent many months negotiating a secret peace with the Germans, the terms of which called for German surrender in Italy and a cease-fire on the Western Front, thus freeing all German divisions for the Russian front. Stalin got wind of this scheme, raised hell with Roosevelt, and Roosevelt wrote back saying he was insulted that the marshal would think he didn't intend to keep his agreements and that Dulles's work was totally unauthorized and unknown to Roosevelt. Al says he's pretty sure Roosevelt was telling the truth, that he'd never heard about what Dulles was up to.

The guys in the Far Eastern Division, the one Al had come out of, had a completely different slant. They tended to think of England as America's chief rival, because England still had India, Burma, and Malaya, while all we had was the Philippines and a foothold in China. One of the topics under discussion in the Far Eastern Division, during the war — and it was seriously talked about — was how could the United States get England to let the Associated Press and the United Press set up bureaus in India and thus break Reuters' monopoly? Seeing England as the potential nemesis was a more traditional governmental view. The War Department's War Plan Red, which was in effect right through the thirties, was a scenario for potential war with England, and covered contingencies like: what would the U.S. do if the English moved the King and/or Queen to Australia?

The European Division and the UN guys split on other issues, too. The biggest bone of contention was the future of the eastern European and Balkan countries on Russia's western border. The Versailles Peace Treaty after World War I had set up pro-Western, anti-Communist democratic governments in all these countries to keep the Russians at bay, and the Russians wanted to make sure that after the Second World War these same countries would have governments sympathetic to Russia so they couldn't do that anymore. The UN contingent didn't see much harm in this switch. The European Division did. Cordell Hull, taking the side of the European Division, had announced himself opposed to "spheres of influence," meaning any area dominated by any major power. Henry Stimson, on the other hand, a Republican who was Roosevelt's Secretary of War during World War II, having once been Hoover's Secretary of State, saw things the way the UN guys did and said he saw no reason why the Russians shouldn't feel secure, because, after all, we had done the same thing way back when by proclaiming the Monroe Doctrine, which said that the Western Hemisphere was off limits to European anti-U.S. influences. Stimson wondered why everyone was so upset.

Shortly after Pearl Harbor, before this all came up, Al tried to leave the State Department to join the army and take up his reserve ROTC commission as a second lieutenant. An assistant secretary of state named Howland Shaw talked him out of it. Shaw also sent memos around the department informing all the young officers that if they did leave State for the army or the navy, they could never come back to State. "The only guy who defied Shaw was Butch Fischer," according to Al, "who left to join the air force. And he was younger than I was and newer to the department. In later years, Butch was general counsel for the Atomic Energy Commission and head of the Arms Control and Disarmament Agency. Which reminds me of Jim Rowe's story about Butch. Jim was a former Holmes secretary, one of the wittiest men in the New Deal, who at one point was *the* top assistant attorney general. When Butch was nominated to be general counsel to the AEC there was, of course, a big FBI background check on him. And two doves, as Donie called them — Donie always called FBI agents doves because they went around in pairs — went to Jim Rowe and said, 'What can you tell us about Mr. Fischer?' Jim said Butch was very able. The agents said, 'Yes we've heard that. What we want to know is if he's so able, presumably he could earn a lot of money. And if he could earn a lot of money, why would he want to work for the government?' The agents were obviously working for the government because they couldn't make a lot of money elsewhere. So it was no good telling them that Fischer just wanted to work for the government.

"So Jim thought for a moment, then hitched his chair closer, and lowered his voice and said, 'I'll tell you something that I've never told anyone.' The agents whipped out their notebooks. Hoover had recently issued an order that all FBI agents had to be either lawyers or accountants. And this was official policy for years even though, in fact, only about 5 percent of the agents ever had LL.B.'s or C.P.A.s. Jim said to the doves, "You're lawyers. You know that the greatest honor that can be given to any lawyer is to be appointed a federal judge. You also know that the only way to get appointed judge is if you put in some work for the party. That's why Mr. Fischer is taking the job.' The agents snapped their books shut, said, 'Thank you very much, sir. This explains everything,' and went off happy."

Al was sent to Yalta as a last-minute replacement for Jimmy Dunn because when Roosevelt saw Dunn's name on the official American list, he crossed it off and said, "Jimmy will ball everything up." The conference, which took place in February 1945 in an old summer resort palace of the Czars, lasted ten days, and, as Al wrote in a letter to Leo Pasvolsky, dashed off flying over Turkey on the way home en route from Moscow to Cairo, "The Crimea Conference was most interesting and *most exhausting*. The secretary had a terrific burden to carry with daily noon meetings with the foreign ministers which carried on through rather lengthy luncheons, after which he had to confer with the President before the daily plenary sessions which began at four o'clock and lasted until eight o'clock or later. Then came tiring and lengthy dinners, which, like the luncheons, called for frequent toasts and constant alertness. We seldom got to bed before two in the morning — in fact, Ed crowded in his consultations with Doc, Chip, and me, his reading of cables from the department and his drafting of cables to the department just before he went to bed or just after he got up in the morning.

"One of the inconveniences of the location was the fact that the three delegations were located in separate villas or houses about three quarters of an hour away by motor from each other. The foreign ministers' meetings alternated between the headquarters of the three delegations. All the plenary sessions were held at Livadia Palace, the American headquarters. You can see that Ed's days — and nights — were pretty full."

Al's big moment at the conference came the day Churchill

hit the ceiling at a meeting discussing the trusteeship provisions of the proposed United Nations, which were at that time referred to as the Associated Nations. As Al wrote Pasvolsky in his letter, "The Associated Nations question caused a lot more trouble. Our British friends were definitely not helpful." Trusteeship was supposed to be a way of dividing up among the Allies administration of defeated German, Japanese, and Italian colonies, as well as parceling out administration of certain other non-self-governing territories that nobody wanted to keep forever. Churchill, however, who liked to say he had not been made His Majesty's First Minister to preside over the dissolution of the British Empire, had the idea that trusteeship was an American ruse to steal India from England, and he got so hot under the collar on the subject that none of his assistants had ever dared explain what the Americans really had in mind. The American and British delegations to Yalta rendezvoused at Malta prior to the conference. And the first question Al had for his British counterparts at Malta was, "Have you explained to the Prime Minister yet about trusteeships?" Anthony Eden said, "No, no. No, no." So the first time Churchill ever heard the details of the American plan was when it was taken up at one of the plenary sessions at Yalta and he didn't listen and got so excited that Roosevelt, who presided over all the sessions, called a recess, while Churchill sat in his chair muttering, "Never, never, never, never."

Harry Hopkins then dashed over to Alger and said, "Can't we drop the subject?" Al said, "No. It's very important to have a policy about what to do with the Japanese territories and the League of Nations mandates." Then Jimmie Byrnes rushed up (Byrnes was at the conference because Roosevelt didn't want him to feel left out, but he didn't have anything to do) and asked Al if he would sit down and write one paragraph explaining what trusteeship was really all about. "So," says Al, "I sat down and on a sheet of yellow foolscap paper wrote an exposition of the important A B C terms, ending up with the phrase that trusteeship applied to 'such other territories as may voluntarily be ceded by any nation.' Byrnes rushed this over to Churchill, who wouldn't even look at it for a moment, finally calmed down, read it, and said, 'Oh, is that all?'

"This draft was then agreed to and it subsequently became part of the UN Charter, almost word for word. If I'd known that was going to happen I would have liked a couple of days to polish it and play with it — not in terms of improving the style, but when you sit down to draft something as important as that, you don't like to think that your first draft will stand, first, last, and always."

There was one boo-boo at Yalta that didn't do anybody any harm in the end — except Al. The conference itself had two major purposes from the American point of view. One was to secure an agreement among all three partners — the U.S., the U.K., and the U.S.S.R. — that could be publicly announced. This was considered extremely important because the Battle of the Bulge had ended just two weeks before the conference and it was felt that any public disagreement at that point might cause German morale to bounce back. The other purpose, which had been pressed on the State Department by the Joint Chiefs of Staff, was that it was vitally important to be nice to the Russians in order to secure their participation in the war against Japan. Russia hadn't, in February 1945, declared war on Japan. The Joint Chiefs didn't know at that moment whether the A-bomb was going to work, and, of course, people like Al didn't even know yet that the A-bomb existed.

The official Pentagon estimate was that the Americans would lose a million lives storming the Japanese islands unless the Russians joined the war. Beyond that, the army was haunted by the fear that when the Americans invaded Japan, the Japanese would spirit the Emperor off to Manchuria, where the strongest Japanese army, the Kwantung army, had been stationed throughout the war in case the Russians ever invaded Manchuria. With the Emperor in Manchuria, the Americans would have to cross the China Sea to get at the Japanese and the war might drag on for years. In the military talks at Yalta, the U.S. and Russia agreed on Russia's declaring war against Japan and signed a secret pact to that effect. In the political talks they reached agreement about the structure of the UN and the final public communiqué of the conference also reported, among other things, an agreement among all parties that the war would be followed by free and open elections in Poland.

There was later an enormous amount of misunderstanding over Poland. I'll let Al explain it: "At an earlier Big Three conference in Teheran, FDR had told Stalin he could help him with a domestic problem by holding a plebiscite in the Baltic states — Russia had swallowed up the Baltics at the beginning of the war. Roosevelt mentioned there were a number of voters in the U.S. from Estonia, Latvia, and Lithuania. Stalin said, 'If you want a plebiscite, of course you can have a plebiscite,' assuming that Roosevelt was talking about window dressing. So when the talk at Yalta came to Poland, in the back of Stalin's mind Roosevelt was talking about the same thing — especially since both Roosevelt and Churchill made special speeches at Yalta, Roosevelt about how many Poles there were in Detroit and Churchill about how the backbenchers in the House of Commons cared a great deal about the Poles and also how the British were host to the Polish government in exile in London. In addition, we probably misled the Russians into thinking that the European Division and its views wouldn't be running things after the war — Roosevelt's own phrase for the European Division was

'Old Dealers' — so the agreement on Poland in the communiqué was really an agreement to disagree, plastered over. This is what power politics is often. And it became clear right after Roosevelt's death that this agreement was paper thin.

"Molotov, on the way to the San Francisco Conference, stopped off at the White House and Truman raised hell about how the London Poles weren't being treated properly, according to the terms of the Yalta agreement. Molotov" — his nickname was "Old Ironpants" — was surprised and said he'd never been spoken to like that before in his life. And that was when Truman said, 'You keep your agreements and you won't be spoken to like that.' This can be called the confrontation that began the cold war.

"Or I could single out other incidents before that, or after it. My own view is the cold war was inevitable, because there were only two people left standing on their feet after the end of World War II, us and the Russians. To the United States it looked as though the world was our oyster, except for those damned Russians. Even at Yalta — could you call it a meeting of three equal partners? Since we and the British had rendezvoused before the conference, that meant that two of the partners had already got their ducks in a row before they even got to the conference. Then, after the war, it was useful to whip up the country to feel nervous about the Russians. This kept labor in its place, kept military appropriations up, kept the army abroad, and maintained an outward thrust to American policy.

"Dean Acheson told me, 'If you don't scare Congress, they'll go fishing.' My reply was, 'If you do scare them, they'll go crazy.' The populace was encouraged to feel jittery, but the people in Washington were never jittery. I don't think Dean ever suffered from a failure of nerve — except perhaps on the day when he began a department conference by describing a 'dream' he had the night before, a dream in which the United States had become encircled by Communist countries. It was right after that 'dream' that he began supporting German rearmament.

"But, look, we acquired military bases all over the world as a result of the war, and if we were going to keep them we had to have a reason for keeping them."

The boo-boo at Yalta had to do with the Russian's desire for two extra votes in the General Assembly of the United Nations, in order to make them feel better about the built-in U.S. majority. They proposed giving votes to two of their constituent republics, the Ukraine and Byelorussia, equivalent, roughly, to giving General Assembly votes to Kansas and Nebraska. The U.S. opposed this, naturally enough, since the UN was supposed to be a club for sovereign nations. One day when Stettinius was briefing Roosevelt about discussions on the subject, he began by saying, "We reached agreement on everything," and before he could say, "Except," Stalin walked in, and Roosevelt said, "My secretary of state tells me they've reached agreement on everything." Stalin said, "Including the two extra votes?" Stettinius said, "But." Roosevelt said, "Sure."

Jimmie Byrnes, when he heard about this agreement, was upset and so was Ed Flynn, the Boss of the Bronx, a friend of Roosevelt's whom he'd also brought along for the ride. Then began a cover-up that Al participated in. Yes, Al was part of a cover-up. The UN guys didn't want word of this agreement to get out, because they hoped to get it rescinded before it was necessary to announce it. Or, failing that, they hoped at least to explain the whole megillah to important senators before it had to come out publicly. The State Department was also giving consideration to a plan to make the deal look better by accepting a Russian proposal to give votes to Alaska and Hawaii, not yet states at that time. Two weeks after the end of Yalta, the story about the two extra votes leaked out anyway. It was printed by Bert Andrews, a Pultizer Prize winner for the *Herald Tribune*, who said this was a secret political agreement of the Yalta Conference and wondered what other secret agreements had been reached. (Nobody at that time, of course, thought secret *military* agreements were a bad thing.) Al says he's always blamed the leak on Jimmie Byrnes — "because I don't know anyone else who would have leaked it." After the leak, Al called up Andrews and bawled him out for gumming things up. Andrews had liked Al up to that point, but he now decided Al was a double-dealer. Three years later he became friends with Chambers and Nixon and had no trouble believing Chambers when Chambers showed him microfilms of State Department papers and said that they'd come from Al.

As secretary-general, or butler, of the San Francisco Conference in May and June of 1945, Al was in charge of several thousand people putting on the show — State Department types, army and navy enlisted men, even a crack team of FBI agents who reported to him daily. "We undoubtedly had a topflight group of FBI people there," Al says now. "We worked together without a hitch." The conference produced the Charter of the United Nations, including Al's trusteeship paragraph, and some fifty nations signed this document. Al and his staff had to make all the arrangements for all fifty nations. The only international airline operating at that time was the U.S. Air Force, so that meant flying everybody in, and there were also hotel rooms, meals, entertainment, girls, chauffeurs, etc., to be taken care of. One of the problems was getting Britain to take India's views seriously. Another problem was cleaning up after Ed Stettinius and Nelson Rockefeller. Stettinius was not a career diplomat. He'd come from big business — U.S. Steel — and he tended to go up to the foreign ministers or prime ministers of small nations and talk to them like junior executives. Nelson did much the same thing, and Al had to go around and smooth a lot of ruffled feathers.

Two of the stories Al used to tell when I was a kid concerned Senator Tom Connally, the head of the Senate Foreign Relations Committee, another nondiplomat. Connally, at a reception, decided to talk to the Dutch foreign minister who was standing across the room, but couldn't remember the man's name. So he yelled out, "Hey, Holland, come over here!" Immediately after Pearl Harbor Connally had a conference with T. V. Soong, the Harvard-educated Chinese ambassador to Washington. Connally slapped Soong on the back and said, "Well, T.V., we'll lick those yellow bastards!"

One of the stories Al told his colleagues after San Francisco was of getting the Russians tickets to the Ice Capades. The Russians enjoyed the show but afterward went down front and put their hands on the ice to make sure that the skaters had really been skating on ice and not just faking the whole thing. Some of the Arabs wanted dates with blondes. Al also had to nudge Truman when Truman, at the end of the conference, got the giggles when the Brazilian foreign minister bowed to him at the moment that a navy aide was whispering in Truman's ear. Al as secretary-general of the conference, was given the honor of flying the Charter back to Washington on a special plane. The Charter was in its own special box attached to its own special parachute. Al was not attached to a special parachute. He says he began to get the idea who and what was important. When he got to Washington, he took the Charter off to the White House and was shown upstairs, where Truman was relaxing and drinking bourbon and branch with some of his pals, including the naval aide who'd whispered in his ear. The President then explained his giggles. The Brazilian foreign minister had been as bald as a billiard ball and the naval aide had whispered, "Pipe the simonize job."

Al was outfoxed twice in San Francisco, first by the French, then by Nelson Rockefeller. The French had not been part of the Yalta Conference and now at San Francisco wanted to show that they were a great power, too, so they requested that all the meetings be translated simultaneously into French — as had been done at the old prewar League of Nations. Al and his staff had hoped to get the UN off to a good start by cutting out the French. So when the foreign minister of France requested translation, Al said he was sorry but there just weren't enough translators available. The foreign minister was prepared for this. He had brought with him all the League of Nations translators who were still alive, and as soon as Al said there weren't any translators, one of these old guys popped up in the back of the room and repeated Al's remark in French. Thereafter, whenever Al said anything, another translator immediately translated that into French. That's how French became one of the official working languages of the United Nations.

Nelson Rockefeller, who'd been coordinator of inter-American affairs and then an assistant secretary of state for Latin American affairs during the war, managed to lobby for enough votes to pass a resolution making Argentina a charter member of the United Nations. Argentina had pointedly not been asked to come to the conference and in fact the original design of the UN seal — the world surrounded by olive branches — worked up before the conference by Oliver Lundquist, a designer and architect and OSS agent on Al's staff, showed a globe that had no Argentina, because Argentina had not only played footsie with the Germans during the war but had become a new home for a number of Germans as the war was drawing to a close.

A final source of annoyance to Al and his pals at San Francisco was John Foster Dulles. Dulles had been made an adviser to the American delegation to the conference because bipartisan support was needed. But Adlai Stevenson, who was in charge of public relations for the American delegation, told Al that every day after Adlai had diplomatically told the press as little as possible about what had gone on that day, Foster would leak everything to them with a Republican twist.

When Al got back to his desk at the State Department after dropping the UN Charter off at the White House, he decided that it was time to get out of government, time to go back to his old Boston law firm, Choate, Hall & Stewart. But Ed Stettinius asked him to stay on at least until the next session of the UN, which was scheduled for the following January (1946) in London. Out of loyalty, Al said, "Sure." Now something entirely unexpected happened. Al got a call from the commandant of a naval cadet program in Upstate New York where Timmy was enrolled. The program took kids out of high school during the war and gave them a little bit of college and a naval commission after a certain amount of studies, and it seems Tim had been locked up in the brig. Why? Well, he'd gone to the commandant and said he wanted to be let out of the navy because he was gay. Of course, they didn't use that word in those days. And he'd been locked up in the brig. This was the only time Al ever pulled rank as a government official and used his office to gain a personal end. He got Tim transferred to St. Albans Naval Hospital in Long Island and placed under psychiatric care. Tim went off to California shortly after this, and Al didn't hear from him much and didn't know really just where Tim was. Tim started working in TV in its early days as a set designer, and later moved to New York and did the same kind of work. At the time of the Hiss case he got in touch with Al. Tim told Al to put him on the stand because he could make mincemeat of Whittaker Chambers' stories of hanging around the Hiss house in Georgetown late at night with microfilms, but Al told Tim he wouldn't let him testify and risk the chance that the prosecution would bring up Tim's past. After Al went to the can Tim decided to become a doctor. He now practices out West, and has four kids.

The next unexpected thing that happened to Al was that on the boat to England for the UN Conference Foster Dulles offered him a job as president of the Carnegie Endowment for International Peace, a New York foundation. Foster had been asked to become chairman of the Endowment and had said he would take the job if they would also hire someone else to do the work and make the other guy president. Al was very interested despite the fact that Foster Dulles had been up to tricks at San Francisco. Why was he very interested? "That's a good question," he said when I asked him. "I don't have an answer to that one. I guess I thought Foster's trickiness at San Francisco was trickiness as a Republican, not personal trickiness, and after all, the Endowment was a respectable organization and I was interviewed for it by John W. Davis, a great lawyer who had been a Democratic candidate for President in 1924, Arthur Ballantine, and another man, Eliot Wadsworth, who was treasurer of the Chamber of Commerce. Foster had a big cackle, but it was a mannerism. He had no sense of humor. I didn't realize he was anything but friendly to me until he took the stand in the last days of my trial, as a witness for the prosecution. I was horrified.

"I guess he was always out for personal advancement, like what he did to his sister, Eleanor. I heard the story about him and Eleanor after I got out of jail. It came from inside the State Department — I've always maintained touch with my friends in the State Department. Eleanor was a very good economist, had come from the Brookings Institute, and had worked her way into a job at the State Department under Truman. Right after Foster was made secretary of state by Eisenhower he called her into his office and said, 'Well,

Eleanor, I've achieved what our father always wanted me to achieve.' Foster's father had told him as a little boy that he should grow up to become secretary of state. Eleanor said, 'Yes, Foster, I hope you're satisfied. We were all sacrificed to your ambitions.' Foster said, 'Eleanor, I think it might be advisable for you to leave the State Department at this point, I wouldn't want to do anything that could cause talk of nepotism.' Eleanor said, 'I earned this job and I'm going to keep it. You want to fire me, fire me. Otherwise, there's nothing left to talk about,' and left the office. Foster did not fire her."

At the London UN Conference, Al got to take Eleanor Roosevelt out to dinner one night. Mrs. Roosevelt was a member of the American delegation. Her appointment had been met with groans on the part of Senators Tom Connally and Arthur Vandenberg. "Oh, Eleanor," they said. She worked very hard at the conference and even left the final reception to finish up some work she had left undone. When she had gone, Vandenberg said, "It hurts me to say this, but there goes a great lady." At which point, Tom Connally said, "Me too . . . me too." The American delegation was housed in Claridge's Hotel in London. The English were on strict rationing at that point, and English people would sometimes bring Mrs. Roosevelt an egg as a present. Once someone brought her a goose egg, which didn't taste very good. Mrs. Roosevelt would invite the Americans in the delegation into her room late at night for scrambled eggs, which they all gobbled, as Claridge's had no eggs. Mrs. R. always felt faintly guilty.

One night, a charming young Belgian baron attached to the Belgian delegation called Al to help him out of a jam — he explained that Paul Henri Spaak, who was at the time either prime minister or foreign minister of Belgium (for twenty ycars Paul Henri Spaak was either prime minister or foreign minister of Belgium), was about to have a birthday, and when they'd asked him what he wanted for his birthday, he wanted Mrs. Roosevelt. Would Al ask Mrs. Roosevelt if she'd come to the party? Al explained the story to Mrs. R. exactly as he had heard it, and she was tickled and said she'd go — "But only if you will be my escort. I don't have an escort these days." He can't remember a thing of what they said to each other at the party but he was thrilled. Partly he can't remember because Mrs. R. spoke French to the Belgians, and all of Al's idioms were dated.

When he got back to the State Department this time, Jimmie Byrnes, who was by now secretary of state — Jimmie Byrnes had begun life as a court stenographer and was later a newspaper owner, a congressman, a senator, a justice of the Supreme Court, director of Economic Stabilization and then director of War Mobilization during World War II, "assistant President," as he was informally known at that time, secretary of state under Truman for a year or two, and then five or six years later governor of South Carolina, in which position, as a champion of segregation in schools, he put up the dough for the losing side in the famous 1954 case in which the Supreme Court decided integration was the law of the land. Anyway, Jimmie, in February 1946, said to Al, "You're in trouble. I've just heard that there's some congressman who's going to make a speech on the floor of Congress saying that you're a Red. I think you ought to do something about this. It all stems from the FBI."

Al said, "Thank you very much, I'll go get in touch with J. Edgar Hoover directly." Al called up J. Edgar Hoover, but Hoover was out of town, so Al went over and saw one of his associates and explained to the man that he had never been a Communist. Then he went back to Byrnes, and Byrnes said, "You did the right thing. I hope this settles it." But it didn't, because rumors about Al began to circulate, although no congressmen made any speeches. Hoover's aide didn't tell Al, but the charges and the rumors all led back to Whittaker Chambers, who, since 1939, had been trying to peddle around Washington the story of Al's having been a Communist, sometimes adding Frank Sayre, Dean Acheson, and Adolf Berle to his list of Reds, depending on his audience. For instance, he didn't say Adolf Berle had been a Communist when he went to Berle in 1939 to tell him Al had been a Commie. The rumors about Al were spread around town in 1946 by Don Russell, a political aide of Byrnes's, who as Byrnes's assistant secretary of state without portfolio had hired a lot of gumshoes to comb through the department officers for security risks. Al never at the time recognized the fact that these guys were security officers — in his mind they were just vulgarians, ward heelers, and political hacks. He didn't even know there were any rumors until Joe Green, a friend of his in the European Division, told him one day that he, Joe, was going around denying rumors that Al was a Red. Al didn't ask Joe who had been calling him names.

Al had been planning to leave the State Department for Choate, Hall & Stewart right after coming back from London, but now he didn't want to leave under a cloud, so he decided to stick around for a few months. That fall, Jack Peurifoy, the guy who had called him from San Francisco the day Roosevelt died, who had become an assistant secretary of state in charge of administration and security, said to him, "Alger, I'm worried about the FBI. They're leaking stuff that is meant to hurt the administration. Hoover must have decided that Truman is going to get licked next year in '48 and is buttering up Dewey. I hate to turn over any security stuff to them, because it's going to get leaked." Al, again, didn't pursue the matter. "I think there was an awful lot of skullduggery going on at the time," Al says now. "But it was mostly over my head, and I can remember this now only in retrospect. As for leaving the government, it was just that I didn't want to give time and energy to policies like the cold war I didn't believe in. After another few months I went in to Dean Acheson and asked him if he thought it was all right for me to leave now at that point, and Dean said, 'Sure.' "

So Al accepted Foster Dulles's job offer and moved to New York and became President of the Carnegie Endowment for International Peace. This was January 1947. Al was the third president of the Carnegie Endowment, which had been founded as a good deed by Andrew Carnegie in 1910, with a grant of ten million bucks. The one proviso Al made before taking the job was that he be allowed to revamp the place and also orient a lot of its work toward support of the UN. The first two presidents of the Carnegie Endowment had been Elihu Root, a statesman from New York, who was secretary of state in Teddy Roosevelt's day, and old Nicholas Murray Butler, the man who was president of Columbia University for forty-three years and turned it into a huge institution by founding a lot of graduate schools. "They were both distinguished old birds who lasted a long time as president," Al says. "I was in and out pretty quickly." Al's secretary at the Endowment, Berthol Sayre, a charming woman with a nasty little dog, had been Butler's secretary, and she used to con Al into making calls on the old man, who had retired as president of Columbia but was still alive and living in the Columbia president's house. Berthol said he was lonely. So Al would go off and take tea and listen to him reminisce about meeting the Kaiser. Al cannot now remember what Butler said to the Kaiser or vice versa.

The Endowment was housed in a little old town house up near Columbia, and the principal achievement of Al's presidency aside from revamping and reorienting was planning a new headquarters building. Most of the Endowment staff hoped he would choose as the new headquarters the old Carnegie mansion on Fifth Avenue, now the Cooper-Hewitt Museum, an enormous pile, with a real pipe organ, a real railroad in the cellar to bring coal to the boiler, and, at the time, an old Scotsman, formerly a chief engineer on a boat, to feed the boiler. The only rooms available in the mansion for offices were maids' rooms. So Al rejected the white elephant, and working with David Rockefeller, one of the trustees of the Endowment, drew up plans for a new office building on First Avenue, just north of what is now the United Nations and was then the proposed site of the United Nations. David Rockefeller's contribution to the project was promising a branch of the Chase National Bank on the ground floor of the building. So the Birchers were right. There *is* a house that Hiss built, in association with international banking interests, a twelve-story gray, stone, and glass building. I've always thought it looks pretty dull. Al has always been very proud of having helped put it up.

Al enjoyed being back in New York, and Prossy seemed to, too. They rented an apartment in Greenwich Village on East 8th Street that overlooked a garden, bringing with them a pussycat named Putter and me, age six. I'm part of this story now, too, and I liked New York myself. Thirty years after the move, mom is still living in the apartment, Al is living about twelve blocks away from it, and I'm living about four blocks away from it in the other direction. Prossy took a job teaching seventh- and eighth-grade English at the Dalton School on East 89th Street, an expensive school with a progressive reputation, and I was put in first grade at Dalton. "It was the proper kind of school for our kind of kookiness," Al says.

Al joined the Harvard Club of New York and was about to be made a member of the Century Club when he got into trouble again in 1948. After he got in trouble he was delisted by *Who's Who in America* and resigned from the Harvard Club and the Metropolitan Club in Washington because he had to spend all his dough on lawyers. His engagement calendar for 1947 shows very few free days. The year was full of meetings, conferences, lunches at the Harvard Club, Metropolitan Club, and Century Club, black-tie dinners, gettogethers with Foster Dulles, trips to Washington, speeches, conferences with Dean Rusk, who had inherited Al's last State Department job. In the back of his engagement book Al listed the cost of out-of-town taxi rides for his expense account and made a rough notation of the Endowment's budget — it came to $400,000 for the year. In the address section of the book he put down "Brooks Brothers, 44th and Madison, sixth floor shop for suits," and on the last page he included a schedule of trains to and from Montpelier, Vermont, for weekends in Peacham, where we were still spending summers, and a list of family birthdays, including Donie's wife, Catherine, and their three kids. There is one entry that reads, "Lunch, Harvard Club, Adlai." Another for Saturday, April 12, says: "Lunch, Tony."

Al often conferred with John W. Davis, a man he considers "the most magnificent man I knew, second to Holmes." Davis was a former solicitor general and a former ambassador to the Court of St. James's, who had three times declined to be on the Supreme Court and had instead gone to work as J. P. Morgan's lawyer. He came from West Virginia, his first case as a young lawyer was the prosecution of a farmer who had stolen an old turkey hen and twenty-nine chickens. King George V referred to him as "the most perfect gentleman I have ever met," and in New York, where he became president of the Bar Association, he was much in demand as an after-dinner speaker because he could tell good stories.

One of the books I've been plowing through is an excellent biography of Davis, *Lawyer's Lawyer* by William H. Harbaugh, on the Alger Hiss recommended reading list on twentieth-century American politics and government. Al also has his own John W. Davis stories — there's the one Davis liked to tell about the day Stanley Reed, Al's old boss and by now a justice of the Supreme Court, joined Davis's golf foursome. Davis was an excellent golfer — Stanley hadn't played much. On the first tee, as Davis prepared to address the ball, Stanley suddenly said, "Mr. Davis, what do you think of Dante?" Davis, without breaking his swing, got off an excellent shot, at the same time remarking mildly, "He has been" — *thwock* — "well spoken of." Davis was seventy-five when Al knew him. He had supported Roosevelt's foreign policy during the war but had had no use whatever for the New Deal, being, in fact, one of the organizers of the anti–New Deal Liberty League which he, along with Al's old Nye Committee antagonists, the du Pont brothers, had helped organize in the thirties. While Al was in jail Jimmie Byrnes, as governor of South Carolina, hired Davis to defend school segregation before the Supreme Court.

In the spring of '47, two doves from the FBI called on Al at his office in Washington and asked him if he was acquainted with a list of names they read out. Some he knew, some he didn't. One of the names was Whittaker Chambers. He told them he hadn't met anyone named Whittaker Chambers, but the name stuck in his mind because he'd known a Bob Chambers, a guy who had been in the AAA and left to join the FBI, and a Tony Whittaker, who had been a classmate of his in law school and had later drawn up the will of old Tom Fansler, Al's father-in-law. In January 1948, Donie called up to say that he'd heard from Eddie Miller, a friend of his, who had been in charge of publicity for the UN at San Francisco along with Adlai Stevenson, that at a New Year's Eve party he'd been to a woman had called Al a Commie, saying that she'd heard this from a *Time* editor named Whittaker Chambers. Eddie had told her to shut up or she'd be sued for libel. Donie later called back and said Eddie had talked to the woman and she wouldn't say things against Al anymore in public, and furthermore she had checked back with Chambers and he said he would keep his mouth shut. The woman's name is Barbara Kerr — I know her, a nice woman. I met her when she was dating former mayor Bob Wagner. She'd once been interviewed for a job at the State Department by Al, which she hadn't gotten, and she hadn't thought much of him as a consequence.

And what was Al's reaction to this incident? "Well, there was a man who seemed to have been sounding off hostilely about me, but he shut up. So what the hell. I'd been called Red and radical too often. If he'd kept on saying it, and saying it too often, and it had become embarrassing, I would have gone to see him. I certainly didn't feel any fear. Maybe that's partly a phobia against fear. Dr. Rubinfine, my analyst, says I have a phobia against fear and don't get afraid even when I should get afraid. I'm also cocky and always optimistic, and God knows I was busy as hell at the time, and it certainly didn't seem important to me."

There were two other occasions when Al wanted to go off to see Whittaker Chambers. The first one came later in 1948 after Chambers opened his mouth again and swore before the House Un-American Activities Committee that Al had been in a Red cell. Al told his boss, Foster Dulles, that he wanted to go right over to Chambers' office at *Time* magazine — by the way, Harry Luce paid all Chamber's legal fees during the Hiss case. But Foster convinced Al that a confrontation would be a no-no. Now, Foster, like J. Edgar Hoover, was expecting Tom Dewey to win the presidential election that November and he was also expecting to become Dewey's secretary of state. He didn't mention to Al that young Congressman Nixon of the Un-American Activities Committee had already dropped around to tell Foster and his brother Allen that Hiss was a hot potato to drop as soon as possible if Foster wanted to save his own skin. No little bell went off in Al's mind to tell him Foster was conning him. After Al got out of jail he wanted to go down to the Chambers farm in Westminster and ask him, "Why did you do this to me?" and demand an apology. Chester Lane, Harvard '30, one of his lawyers, told him it was too late to solve the case that way.

On Monday, August 2, 1948, Al returned to work from a month's vacation in Peacham, and a reporter called up and told him that on the following day Whittaker Chambers would swear before a hearing of the Un-American Activities Committee, called to investigate espionage in government, that he, Chambers, had been a member of a Communist cell in the Agriculture Department in the middle thirties and that other members of the cell had been Lee Pressman, Nat Witt, John Abt, and Alger and Donald Hiss. When, the next day, Chambers did testify, all of Alger's associates at the office and in particular, Chuck Dollard, president of the Carnegie Corporation, told him to ignore the charges, that the House Committee was a thoroughly discredited organization, that Al should relax and enjoy himself.

It was true that the last man the House Committee had tried to nail, an official of the Bureau of Standards, had been thoroughly and convincingly vindicated just a few weeks before. It was also true, as the chairman of the Un-American Activities Committee, J. Parnell Thomas, later admitted, after he himself got out of jail (he was nailed for kickbacks), that the hearings were called solely to discredit Democrats as part of the '48 Republican drive on the White House. And the hearings weren't getting anywhere until Al came along because up to that point none of the Democrats fingered ever rose to the bait and stopped in to protest their innocence. Al's reaction, of course, as we all know, was to ignore the advice and hotfoot it down to Washington and deny Chambers' charges under oath. He was the only one of the men named by Chambers who chose this course, including Donie. Donie later denied the charges before the committee too, but only after Al had himself insisted on going on the record.

It was not the last time that Al ignored advice in the next few months. When Al testified, he challenged Chambers to repeat his remarks outside of a congressional hearing, saying if he did so, Al would slap a libel suit on him. Under the law, nothing you swear to before a congressional hearing is libelous. Like Al, Donie was no longer working for the government anymore — he'd joined Covington & Burling, where he was becoming a tariff expert. And the smart boys at C & B told him never sue anyone for libel. It's more trouble than it's worth even when you're right, and even if you win the whole process and get damages you look bad. It's overkill. Donie passed this advice on to Al. Al didn't take it. It was as a result of the libel lawsuit Al did slap on Chambers when he repeated his insults on "Meet the Press" that Chambers, his back to the wall, produced the famous Pumpkin Papers: the typewritten copies, and a little later the microfilms, of old government documents that Dick Nixon, with Bert Andrews' help, immediately called "proof of the most treasonable plot in the history of the Republic," even though they were either file-and-forget State Department papers circulated around a lot of offices or available-to-the-public navy Department memos about what color to paint the fire extinguishers.

Of course, Dick never let anyone see the microfilms with the fire extinguisher memos, he just let the press take pictures of him holding the microfilm. Republican newspapers reprinted some of the other documents. Al's pal Charlie Darlington, going home from work one night, was astonished to find on page one of his evening paper a long background memo he'd written ten years before and forgotten. "The style is good," he told his wife when he got home, "although I suppose I could have said the same thing in half as many words. You know, if I'd taken that thing to the Washington *Post* ten years ago and offered them a thousand dollars to print it, they'd have laughed in my face."

After the Pumpkin Papers were produced, Al was asked to testify before a grand jury. John W. Davis advised him not to testify, pointing out that if he didn't, which he had a right not to, he could never be indicted. But Al wanted to testify before the grand jury. "So what did you think you were doing at the time when you weren't taking advice?" I asked Al. "I had a little of the feeling of Saint George and the dragon," he said. "I wanted to be the hero. I thought right up to the last minute it would turn out right. And I still think if I'd had the breaks, if I'd known then what I know now, if the climate had been different, it would have turned out right. I went down to deny the charges — well, in the first place, the difference between Chambers' charges as related by someone else at a New Year's Eve party and before the House Committee was the difference between the unofficial and the public and the official. I was trained to be very official-minded, and to pay no mind to loose talk. It seemed important to challenge these charges in the same forum in which they were uttered, and to respect an official committee of Congress. Of course, I didn't realize then what shits they were. And then I just couldn't believe that anyone wouldn't love me, once I was there. And in fact, the hearings at first seemed to bear that out and go my way. Right up until the Pumpkin Papers, I was in clover. Also, I was being accused of disloyalty, and I have never been disloyal. And I like to think it is part of my characterology, when stones fall on my head I try to make something of the stones — a cairn, at least. Old Doctor Shotwell, my number two at the Endowment, used to say: if you can't do something about it, do something with it. When I was finally indicted I wasn't unhappy. I welcomed a chance to go into court, the setting in which I felt happiest, and disprove everything."

Al had two trial lawyers in his two trials, Lloyd Paul Stryker in the first trial, who had the reputation of being the best criminal lawyer in the country — he was a friend of John W. Davis's and had been recommended to Al by Felix Frankfurter — and Claude B. Cross of Boston in the second trial. Al got rid of Stryker for two reasons. One, he didn't like Stryker's style or approach. Stryker concentrated on Chambers in the first trial and not on the documents, yelling dramatically at the jury that Chambers was a moral leper who should be preceded into court as lepers had been in medieval times by someone shouting, "Unclean! Unclean!" The other reason was that after the trial ended in a hung jury, Stryker told Al he could go on getting him a hung jury forever, and this wasn't good enough for Al. Al was much more pleased with Cross's presentation in the second trial because he thought Cross did a thorough and painstaking job of explaining all the documents. Al wasn't surprised when one of the reporters covering the case came up to him after the jury had filed out to deliberate and said, "Do you want to know the verdict of the press? Not guilty — in fifteen minutes." Even when, a few days later, the verdict came in — guilty — he wasn't discouraged and told the lawyers that they had just begun to fight. The lawyers gave him strange looks. The judge in the first trial, Sam Kaufman, reprimanded Al for snickering in court as the jury was being chosen from a select list of gas and electric company foremen and told him that a trial was a serious business. According to Helen Buttenwieser, one of Al's lawyers, the only time she's ever seen him completely shocked was after the first hung-jury verdict. The vote was eight to four against Al in the jury, and he couldn't believe that even eight people would disbelieve him.

His attitude toward Chambers during most of the two trials was that the man was a nut, out for fairy vengeance. Before the first trial, columnist Joe Alsop had called up Al's lawyers to tell Al to read *The Class Reunion,* a book by Franz Werfel that Chambers had translated. It's the story of a man who has an unreciprocated crush on another man named Adler and later betrays him. Al was eager to have psychiatrists testify to this effect at the trial. "I was very much interested in psychoanalysis," he said to me recently, "because of Prossy. I mean, because she had been in analysis with a student of Freud's as a young woman, for a year, and I thought I was very knowledgeable. I had read *The Interpretation of Dreams* and at the Carnegie Endowment I had met Dr. Carl Binger and Dr. Frank Fremont-Smith, the father of the book reviewer. They were both interested in trying to arrange to have world leaders psychoanalyzed as a way of improving the international situation. You can imagine how our conversations had gone back and forth. I would say things like, 'Even sensible leaders who start out as straight as a die couldn't resist pressures for war until there are innovative structural reforms in all political systems.' Obviously, Binger was half right, and I was half wrong." Binger did testify at the second trial, but Tom Murphy, the prosecutor, an assistant United States attorney who hadn't been getting anywhere in the U.S. Attorney's Office and had been about to resign from the department until the Hiss case came along, made mincemeat out of Binger's testimony by making Binger sound sick for thinking about such things and suggesting that talk about psychosis was creepy, a smear, and the act of desperate men.

Sam Kaufman, the judge, was reassigned to another case before the second trial, largely because Dick Nixon called for his impeachment because Kaufman's jury had failed to convict. The new judge, Henry Goddard, had been appointed to the bench by Warren Gamaliel Harding. He was an old-time Republican pol who invited Alice Roosevelt Longworth, Teddy Roosevelt's daughter, and her sister and her niece to sit up front with the lawyers in court during the trial, not behind the lawyers with the rest of the spectators. They came every day and knitted and the niece made sketches and they all grinned every time Murphy made a good point and frowned every time Cross made a good point. They had seats on one side of the courtroom so they were always directly facing the jury.

Goddard routinely napped on the bench during testimony. It came out during the trial that one of the jurors was the wife of a bailiff of another judge before whom, between the two trials, Al and his lawyers had asked to have the site of the second trial shifted to Vermont — this judge had denied that motion. A juror with a connection to a case is standard grounds for a mistrial, but Cross, when Goddard asked him what he wanted to do about it, said he would leave the matter up to His Honor, and His Honor didn't want to do anything about it. It came out after the trial that the forelady of the jury attended an Episcopal Church where Goddard was a vestryman, and equated him with God. And it's now come out in the FBI files on the case that were released to Al last year that the FBI knew all along that two other jurors in the second trial had relatives in the Bureau. An FBI memo says that when the Bureau so informed the prosecution, they "requested that it be kept quiet."

Even so, Murphy was worried until the end. When the second trial jury was out and sent back for further instructions, he groaned, slumped over his table in the courtroom with his head on his arms, and said, "The damn, dumb bastards, if they can't agree on it this time, I'll never try this case again." But of course they did agree, and the victorious Murphy was later appointed police commissioner of New York by Mayor Vincent Impellitteri and is today a Federal District judge.

People on all sides of the case agreed that Al's demeanor as defendant and witness seemed curiously detached. Judge Kaufman said later that he thought Alger was innocent of the charges in the perjury indictment against him — there were two counts in the indictment: one had to do with the dates Al and Chambers had known each other, which was important because the documents Al was supposed to have turned over to Chambers were dated long after they had stopped seeing each other, and the other charge, of course, was simply Al's denial that he had ever given papers to Chambers. Kaufman said that he thought Chambers had told more than the truth and Al less than the truth. But he said he thought Al was an honest man. He added, however — he was talking to one of Al's lawyers who later did some work for him on another matter — that he "couldn't say the same for Mrs. Hiss."

Now Prossy did not make a good witness. She was very nervous, and Murphy scored points when he asked her if she'd ever been a member of the Socialist Party. She said, no, and he then produced an application for membership. I have found it very interesting to discover, in talking to people associated with the case, how many people on all sides of the case thought that the real truth was that Al was innocent but was covering up for something Prossy had done. In addition to Judge Kaufman, several of Al's own lawyers believed in their heart of hearts that this was what had really happened, and one of the top FBI men investigating the case thought exactly the same thing.

John Smith, who published *Alger Hiss, The True Story* in 1976, came up with one explanation for this widespread belief, namely, that Al *was* covering up, not for any Commie crimes by Prossy, but by suppressing that old abortion of hers and at the same time making sure Tim's gay episode didn't get on the record. John's story is true enough — as far as it goes. Prossy *was* worried about the abortion becoming public knowledge, and Al refused to put Tim on the stand because Tim had found out that some of his friends were being closely questioned by the FBI. Tim, if he had testified, could of course have denied Chambers' stories about popping over to the Hiss house and banging on the door in the middle of the night on a regular basis to receive papers. And Al has all along thought that if the case had been tried in Washington instead of in New York, it would have been laughed out of court, because for one thing a Washington jury would know that you don't come around Georgetown in the middle of the night making noise without all the neighbors complaining. And for another thing they would have realized that the house Al was living in during his supposed spyhood was one of those little Georgetown places where everybody always knows what everybody else is up to.

The house in question was one of three houses in a row that had been put up as cheap housing for nurses during the Civil War — Louisa May Alcott once lived there. When Al was shaving in the morning he could talk, if he felt like it, to the man in the next house shaving on the other side of the mirror. There was no trouble in the building because all three families were quiet. The Chambers story, as presented at the trials, was that he came over at ten at night, got the papers, took the train to Baltimore, had them photographed there, came back to Washington around two or three in the morning, and gave them back to Al. Another family in the row was the Robb family. Al remembers the birth of their "charming baby boy. We little suspected that he would grow up to marry a daughter of a President." That was Chuck Robb, who married Lynda Bird Johnson.

Well, as I was saying, John Smith is right in a way — Al was participating in a sort of cover-up for Prossy's feelings. The charges of disloyalty to the country for which he was on trial weren't always uppermost in Al's mind during his trials —he considered the charges "bullshit" and assumed that a courtroom examination of them would clear them up immediately. He was more concerned about being personally loyal to Prossy. Loyalty was always a key word in their marriage. Shortly after they got hitched they went to a party at the house of Bill Marbury, a Baltimore lawyer and one of Al's cohorts, and Al spent the evening with his pals while Prossy sat in the corner feeling neglected. Driving home she told him his conduct was "disloyal," and as soon as she said this Al promised never to leave her alone again. Al kept up with Marbury over the years, but mostly at lunchtime, and when he sued Chambers for libel in the fall of 1948 retained Marbury as his counsel. One night in December 1948, after a weekend on the Eastern Shore, Al and Prossy drove over to the Marburys, and after dinner Marbury told Al he was likely to be indicted. This was the first time anyone had said this to either Al or Prossy, and Prossy "went into a panic," as Al describes it now. "At first she was stunned in a way I'd never seen before, but that didn't surprise me because I was just as surprised at the news as she was. Then as soon as we were alone she reacted with great anxiety about what would happen if Bill were right. She wondered if she'd be indicted and how the trial would be paid for. Soon she began to ask less practical and more imaginative questions. 'Will Tony be able to stay in school? Will I be able to continue teaching? Will we be able to keep the car?' " Prossy remained this way almost continuously, and in fact nothing Al could do or say between that night and March 21, 1951, more than two years later, when he went off to jail, could ever stop her from being overanxious and on occasion hysterical for more than an hour or two at a time. Here's what Al told me about this subject when it came up the other day:

"When the Pumpkin Papers came out, my first reaction was,

this is just another goddamned explosion I'll have to cope with and contend with. Nothing ever happened that year, it seemed, without the press boiling after me. I had no idea what was really on those Pumpkin Papers until my lawyer, Ed McLean, my old friend from law school, got ahold of them, and then I could see right away that they were phonies — phonies in the sense that they didn't come from my office or from me, except for three cables that anyone could have taken. Nixon waved the films at the press without letting the press read them, and then he came up to New York and waved them again at the grand jury and the indictment was really based on those microfilms. During the trials, they proved to be so irrelevant, so unconnected to me, Murphy really dropped them and concentrated on the typewriter stuff, trying to prove that Chambers' papers had been typed on one of the old typewriters I'd once owned, that the characters on them were identical with those on old letters and memos of Prossy's that certainly had been typed on that machine. Of course, Murphy during the trial was willing to say officially that there was no way of telling, even if they had been typed on the same machine, who the typist had been. And I was doubly outraged by the sonofagun when in his summation at the end of the second trial he invited the jury to look for similar typing errors in Chambers' documents and the old letters Prossy had typed.

"Now, of course, Prossy never quit her job. She continued to cook and look after you. She remained loyal and affectionate. She was helpful, tried to get up a calendar of events of all the things we'd done so we could check our stories against the stories Chambers was telling. And after the second trial, she spent a whole summer indexing the case up in Peacham. Did a remarkable job. Part of her panic probably had to do with the fact that she thought of herself as a Quaker, and for Quakers a trial is an impropriety where you are at the mercy of vulgar, staring people. In Lewisburg and for years afterward, I blamed myself for not having taken the time before the trials to take her down to a courtroom, show her it was not a frightening place to be. For me, of course, it was a sanctuary, and on the first day of the first trial she said to me, 'I had no idea it would be so quiet.' Then another way of looking at it is that Nixonism/McCarthyism affected a million or more people, if you include all the families, so there were a lot of frightened people in the country.

"Now I, myself, was not frightened. As Helen Buttenwieser said to me once, 'Alger, you know, you don't terrorize easily.' But Prossy did go into a type of collapse. I tried to impart courage to her. I didn't catch fear from her. I'd always known that she frightened easily. When we were driving in the car she would get in a dither at a crossroad and not know which road to take, and when she started to plan a vacation she'd write to ten different places and then get tense and be unable to decide on any of them. I never paid much attention to that — I put Prossy on something of a pedestal: I thought she was very sophisticated; she was a divorcee, and she'd been analyzed in New York in the twenties by a lady analyst who had studied with Freud and who kept flying squirrels in her house; at the same time I liked to think our marriage was one of perfect equality; and I also had in me the old southern thought that all women were 'flighty' — but once my old friend Bill Marbury said, 'Alger, you're going to be indicted,' there was this constant, I guess I'd call it 'free-floating,' anxiety that it was impossible to calm. If you eliminated one damned thing, talking rationally and reasonably, there was always another. God, it was burdensome to go over her anxieties at length.

"Every day seemed a new wound to her. One blow after another. I felt I wasn't getting across. And, by God, the last thing I wanted after a long day with the lawyers was a long anxious talk session with Prossy, when I would have enjoyed sleeping or reading or being loving. We started getting a lot of crank calls, many of them in the middle of the night, and there was a long time when whenever the phone rang, I jumped. But Prossy got into a near paranoid state, I guess I'd call it. She believed the walls of our apartment were bugged. Well, maybe they were, but when I'd get home after a long day she'd want to take a long walk to talk. And I'd do it, although it didn't seem to change anything. At the same time, I constantly believed that she'd get better, and as far as I was concerned, it was essential before anything else that she be supported through this very terrifying experience.

"This was the priority. Loyalty is a very big thing in my life. I'd been brought up on stories of the Knights of the Round Table, and then loyalty is an old southern tradition — something I think I couldn't ever get through to Mike Zeligs when I was talking to him. He always thought it was just me. But this is one way in which Southerners are different from Yankees. Loyalty was all the Confederacy had when it went down. When I met Arabs at San Francisco, I was quite frankly fascinated by them because I saw in their traditions the same fierce loyalty to family and clan. She was dependent on me, and I had to support her. It was on my mind all the time.

"When I got back from jail I suggested that we not be so closely entwined, that we each have independent activities. I said I had to speak more frankly. She would not accept suggested changes. She said any change was disloyal to the noble, splendid, beautiful ideals we'd shared. The first night I got home the bed collapsed merely by my sitting on it. She had kept it together by wrapping it with string. I thought this was pretty funny and told the story. She didn't like my telling it. Then I found you having all that anxiety about your homework every night, staying up until one or two in the morning in eighth grade to get your homework done. I thought that Prossy was pressuring you, as a teacher's son, to do better. And that was shortly after you'd fallen and knocked your front teeth out — for the second time. And you told me you kept having urges to jump in front of subway trains and jump off the balcony of Carnegie Hall. That was a real red signal.

"Before, when you were little, I thought she'd merely been spoiling you. That didn't seem all that harmful to me. Now I thought that to save you from tension you damned well ought to go off to Putney School. When I told her this, she accused me of trying to seduce you. Of course, the trials also meant the abasement of Prossy. The whole time we were in Washington, it was a nuisance for her being alone a lot, but she was Mrs. Hiss at the diplomatic dinners, and part of a very happy, jolly group. She played four-hands piano, quartets and trios with Tel Taylor, Katherine Stanley-Brown, and others, and when we moved to New York she was the president — I mean the wife of the president — of the Carnegie Endowment. And when I went away 'disgraced' she lost all status. But I also think she'd already interpreted Tim's episode when she heard about it in 1945, as some kind of inner disgrace for her.

"Later, when you were at Harvard, I came to think that she exaggerated your troubles — maybe even relished them, because if you were in trouble then she could help you. She was constantly saying what terrible shape you were in. Then I'd come up and see you, and you were fine. I'd tell her you were fine and she'd tell me I was heartless, that I didn't know what you were going through."

I think I can understand what was happening to dad and mom from the feelings in my own memory. When dad would come visit me at college the future would often tend to look like a more reliable proposition than when mom was up for a visit. And it was the same thing when I was a kid during the

Hiss case. When I'd talk to dad about the trials they sounded sort of interesting. When I'd talk to mom about them they were a waking nightmare. That's one part of it. The other is I can remember dad reasoning with mom. He always addressed himself to whatever specific question she was pressing at the moment — Where will we get money if you go to jail? Will we have to give up the apartment? Things like that. It was almost like they were discussing funeral arrangements. But I don't think either one of them at the time quite understood what was on the other's mind. Mom thought dad's message for her was "He agrees with me. This is the end of the world for us. But he's telling me that because we're civilized people we have to arrange our own disgrace calmly." But what Al was saying was, "No matter what happens we'll still be alive, won't we? That's the only thing."

After all, the only people who can make funeral arrangements are survivors. I don't think they ever got this point straightened out. I asked Al recently if he'd agree with me that maybe he went to jail to get away from Prossy. "She definitely did the best she could during the huge strain of the trial," he said. "In retrospect, with all the recent disclosures of FBI telephone tapping, bugging, and even burglaries, her concern about the difficulty of obtaining any privacy in our talks doesn't seem paranoid at all. On this point I was the one to be faulted for my everlasting assurance that we were in the best hands — the courts — and everything would work out O.K. Perhaps by the time I went in I could see certain advantages to a period of separation in which we each could think through the emotional problems that the trial had exacerbated. I was not altogether horrified."

6. Alberto

WITHIN TEN MINUTES after Al's conviction, legal procedure required him to swear an oath that he wouldn't jump bail. He considered this an odd procedure for someone whose word had just been publicly branded false. A few days later, he was given the maximum sentence on each count, the two sentences to run concurrently. As it turned out, he served three years and eight months. He was denied parole and the prison authorities wouldn't give him meritorious good time or prison industry good time, two supposedly automatic procedures designed to knock a little time off your sentence if you behaved yourself and did the work assigned you. But they had to give him adjusted time (statutory good time) and that took sixteen months off the sentence.

Before Al went off to the jug — and he didn't enter prison until March 21, 1951, over a year after he was convicted — he started boning up on what he was in for, partly because I started asking him what it was going to be like and whether he would have a chance to play baseball, partly because Al is Al. He wasn't afraid but he was curious. All that he knew about jail he had learned from *New Yorker* cartoons, and he imagined himself wearing striped clothes and breaking up rocks all day. He even thought about, as he now says, "the interests, I'm frank to admit, of a new world, new interests, a new challenge."

It's funny but different people who were nailed by the House Committee or Nixon or Hoover or Joe McCarthy — and Joe McCarthy didn't even get into the anti-Communist line until two weeks after Al was convicted — reacted in different ways. Some people went all to pieces, other people did different things. Jack Service, bounced from the State Department as one of the guys made to take the fall for the fall of China, made a million bucks making steel gadgets. Lionel Stander, a gravelly voiced character actor, when he was called before the House Committee, announced in advance that he would name names. This was what the committee loved best, and he was greeted with anticipation. Then he told the congressmen he would name the names of the most un-American people he knew, and named every member of the committee. They hustled him out immediately without asking him any questions. He was blacklisted, of course, but he went to Wall Street and made half a million dollars playing the market.

Little things happened to other people. Helen Buttenwieser, one of Al's New York lawyers, said that people she hadn't liked much anyway stopped talking to her. Her husband, Ben, a big New York banker, was not elected head of the New York United Fund because his wife had been a lawyer for Alger Hiss, and he was almost kept off the board of directors of the New York Philharmonic for the same reason. Their oldest son, Larry, was not elected president of the American Civil Liberties Union branch at the University of Chicago Law School because of his mother. The FBI tried to keep their second son, Peter, out of a Harvard summer teaching program in Africa. In the sixties, their youngest son

Paul's medical commission as a captain in the U.S. Army medical corps was held up a year while FBI doves asked everyone he knew questions about his mother.

The legal fees for Al's trials ran to about a hundred grand. He used up his savings — which didn't amount to much, since he'd only started saving when he took the Endowment job. Donie went into hock for about twenty grand and spent the next decade paying it off. Minnie asked everyone she knew in Baltimore for money and generally showed more interest in Al than she had when he'd been doing all right. The rest of the money came from friends or well-wishers, many of whom Al had never even met. "If this thing had to happen," Al says, "it couldn't have come at a better time. I was still young and had my health, but I'd been a lawyer long enough so that I had close friends who were themselves by that time skilled and experienced lawyers and they volunteered part-time help. And the full-time lawyers for me worked for minimum fees. If the case had come up a dozen years before it would have been difficult to make it."

Alger went to a fellow New Dealer for advice about jail — Austin McCormick, former deputy director of the Federal Prison Bureau and later, for many years, head of the only prisoners' aid society convicts then had any respect for, the Osborne Association, named after Thomas Mott Osborne, an enlightened warden of Sing Sing. Nowadays prisoners think the Fortune Society is also on their side. McCormick had served six or seven voluntary prison terms to see what it was like, under his own name, because the first time he went in, under an assumed name, the prisoners all tumbled to who he really was within a day and he was treated worse because they thought he was a spy. The inmates were able to detect him because any jail is basically run by its inmates, who do all the steno-clerical work, as well as all the hard work. In New Deal days McCormick had once gone to a cocktail party at

Al and Prossy's house. Vi Bernard, a psychiatrist friend of Al and Prossy's who had researched Carl Binger's testimony at the trials, set up an appointment with McCormick, and Al said to himself, if I were a nineteenth-century traveler about to set out for Arabia and somebody asked me if I'd like to see Doughty, I'd be very pleased.

McCormick, who worked out of an old office on East 30th Street in New York, wised Al up and even told him exactly which prison he'd be sent to. The rule of thumb in the federal prison system is that you're supposed to be sent to the federal prison nearest your home. But the nearest prison to New York is in Danbury, Connecticut, a place that has a reputation as a country club, and McCormick told him he'd never be sent there. At the same time, McCormick said, Al wouldn't be sent to Atlanta, a joint considered too rough for political prisoners. McCormick predicted Lewisburg, a maximum security prison built during the New Deal, outside Lewisburg, Pennsylvania, a town fifty miles north of Harrisburg and the home of Bucknell College. McCormick forecast that Al wouldn't make parole or be allowed to earn meritorious or prison industry good time. He asked Al what kind of job he'd like to get inside, and Al said he thought he might volunteer for the prison hospital. McCormick said, "Don't do it. You'll have access to drugs there, and you'll be living with people who will want drugs, and they'll ask you to get them, and you'll be in the middle. You'll either get yourself in trouble violating the rules for your new friends, or you won't get the drugs and your new friends won't like you. And in any case, you won't be doing anyone any good."

Al said he'd like to do some teaching in that case. McCormick said, "No, they won't let you teach. They'll say you're teaching Communism, even if you're teaching mathematics, and they'll be afraid of what someone like Walter Winchell will say." Al said, "How about the library?" Mc-

Cormick said, "No, that's too easy. They'll send you to the storeroom" — which is what happened. The storeroom was double-locked, so the authorities could say they had Hiss in a completely secure situation, but the real reason for double-locking the storeroom doors was to keep the guards from pilfering plumbing and electrical supplies, and stationery.

Al heaved stuff around all day, occasionally being asked to help unload sides of beef for the kitchen, and once or twice he got a chance to snag a couple of steaks destined for the officers' mess. Sometimes he had to carry supplies to the solitary confinement cells known as "the hole" and "the new hole" — so called because the only facilities are a round hole in the middle of the floor toward which everything slopes. Al enjoyed storeroom work, as it turned out, because moving things around was something real to do, as well as good exercise, and the guard in charge of the place, Mr. Grove, a local man with whom he got to be good friends, let him read books when there was nothing else to do. From the storeroom he could see all the new prisoners arriving and all the men who'd done their time going home.

McCormick's advice was "You'll be the new boy in school and you'll have a lot to learn. The others will all be experienced upperclassmen. Listen and learn. That's the best advice I can give you." Al himself found prison not unlike college. As he told me in 1973, the first time he and I ever talked about such things, "I suppose I learned as much in my forty-four months there as I learned in three years at Harvard. In college you're supposed to learn book learning, social relationships, maturity. Jail was the same kind of educational experience, the only difference was we didn't get summer vacations." One day in the Lewisburg yard, another guy asked him what he thought of the people in there. And Al said he thought they were interesting. The guy said, "Interesting? What the hell does that mean?" Al said, "I mean I like them." The guy said, "Oh, why didn't you say so? That's different."

One way and another, Al learned a lot. The first things to learn were manners. At one time after he got out he thought about writing a manual of etiquette for political prisoners. "This I would recommend to anyone entering the federal prison system. I learned to keep my mouth shut. And I learned the ways of living in a joint, quite different from living outside. The first day I was there I was told never speak at breakfast. Everyone's got his own problems, and the guy next to you may be in a rage. Maybe he's had a 'Dear John' letter from his wife, or his lawyer has written saying there's no hope. I also learned, never pass bread with your fingers because the other guy can't be sure you haven't just been removing clinkers from your asshole." All this advice from McCormick and fellow inmates Al followed meticulously. He kept his nose clean in the can, and when William Remington, who worked in the hospital and was in prison for the same offense — namely, denying espionage charges, was murdered two weeks before Al was set for release by a real McCoy, one of the Tennessee Hatfields and McCoys, Al had the smarts to refuse the warden's offer of a special guard at his side. He didn't want the other inmates who had become his friends to think he'd asked the authorities for protection.

Before Al was sent off to Lewisburg, he spent a few weeks at West Street, the old federal detention center in New York, which finally closed down in 1975. A visitor sat on one side of a desk and the prisoner on the opposite side. There was a large piece of plate glass between them, and to talk each person had to pick up a telephone. Facilities for the prisoners were equally antiquated. As Al said, "It was really like a zoo, because it was made up of iron cages. There were eight or a dozen men in a single cage, double-decker bunks. The top man couldn't really straighten up because there were bars overhead and bars all around. Bright lights on all night, the radio announcing calls blaring right over your head.

"The first night I was there, I hate to say this because it sounds too corny, but it happened to be Holy Thursday, three days before Easter, and I thought of Sam Ditta, the man who was sleeping above me, as the suffering servant. In the middle of the night, Sam — he was from New Orleans — suddenly screamed, and I thought he was having a bad dream about being in jail. He sat up in bed and banged his hand and he said, 'I thought I was drawing a catfish out of the bayou.' In his dream he'd jerked his hand up and hit the bar over his head. Well, that scream woke us all up so we sat around talking. Sam said, 'I knew as soon as I got into court and the clerk read out: "The United States of America against Sam Ditta," I didn't have a chance. The whole United States against poor little Sam.' Sam had been caught for moving a stolen automobile across state lines. He'd bought the car on time, and he was married to the sheriff's daughter, and the sheriff hadn't approved of the marriage, and apparently under the law of Louisiana, if you're buying a car on time and you haven't fully paid for it yet, you're not supposed to drive it out of the state. So when he drove it out of the state, the sheriff saw a chance to break up the marriage."

Al himself, in bed at night, often went through replays of the trial in his head, trying to think of places where if he'd only asked the right questions he could have trapped Chambers or Mrs. Chambers in a lie. For a long time, day and night, a line from *King Lear* kept running through his head. " 'Tis the times' plague, when madmen lead the blind."

Lewisburg is a red brick Gothic pile set out in the middle of farmland. One of its façades, as Al noted right away, is modeled on Hampton Court Palace in England. Pheasants occasionally fly over the wall around the jail. The prison population in the early fifties numbered 1500 to a couple thousand. The breakdown was one-third army prisoners, kids who had been convicted of civilian crimes in Germany, Austria, and Italy, and given stiff sentences by the military authorities in order to reassure the local population; one-third hillbillies, as they were known, kids from the small towns and hills of Kentucky and Tennessee, mostly inside for robbing banks and stealing cars for joy rides; the other third Italians from the New York area, who, as Al said, ran the joint. Alger was given prison number 19137.

The procedure was for the first month you were in quarantine, a kind of solitary confinement whose official purpose was to keep the new prisoners from spreading communicable diseases, but whose real purpose was, as Al says, to bore you to death and let you know that the authorities have the upper hand. For the first ten days you couldn't buy toothpaste or cigarettes. You were allowed to read, which was not most of the guys' idea of fun, but Al had a good time and spent the month reading *Don Quixote*, a book he found in the library that he'd never had time for before. After this month prisoners — by the way, the prison uniform was gray flannelette shirt and blue jeans or khakis, not striped clothes — were moved into dormitories, sixty beds to a room.

At night they could listen to the radio on headsets. There was a choice of two stations. "The programs were 'This is Your FBI,' 'Gangbusters,' sitcoms, things of that sort. And the fights. Any time there was a prize fight you could get that. And hillbilly music on the other channel. I'm not against country music, even that didn't turn me against it. But once lights were out at ten o'clock, it was eerie to hear laughter for no known cause, if you didn't have your headset on. You'd hear it breaking out all over the dormitory. You know, when people start laughing about something you don't know that's funny, it's very peculiar. And these ripples of unprovoked laughter would ramble on in the dormitory until the radio was turned off."

There was strict segregation at Lewisburg at the time. The blacks had their own dormitories and ate on a different side of the dining hall from the whites, although the prison industries were integrated and blacks and whites all went out for exercise together in the yard. Black Muslims were just beginning to appear in the prison population — nine or ten of them at Lewisburg at that time. The whites all thought they'd latched on to a smart new gimmick for getting special privileges — the Christians and the Jews had chaplains and rabbis and the Muslims were demanding a Muslim spiritual leader and time off for worship services.

Al was generally well liked and respected by inmates, civilian employees, and guards alike, all of whom had heard about him and wanted to meet him as a celebrity. It was said that they probably would have asked for his autograph if they'd had a piece of paper. And it was noted that Al would talk to anyone, murderer, car thief, whatever. Al met brothers of guys he'd gone to high school with in Baltimore. He even met one guy with a grudge against him, the Celluloid Kid from Washington, who had been sent to jail for robbing Donie's house. "What kind of guy are you?" said the Celluloid Kid. "Your brother turned me in." Al had already been tipped off about this guy by Donie and knew how to handle him. "I've heard the whole story," he said. "You were certainly very careless. My brother wasn't even in the city at the time, it was your own sloppy procedures that got you nabbed." The Celluloid Kid said, "You're the wrong kind."

And there were guys like Radar, a hillbilly with big ears, and Tiny, the giant lifer who had been there since the place was built, and who would never get out. Tiny had a placid disposition and wouldn't react when the kids in the place ragged him except one day when he threw a guy who had been after him for months down a flight of stairs and killed him. Everyone understood — they all sympathized with Tiny. The prisoners who were most unpopular were the middle-class businessmen who had six-month sentences for income tax evasion and spent their entire sentences bitching and complaining: "I had it all fixed with the D.A. How come my brother didn't get it? My uncle's been doing this for years." The one guy no one could stand was David Greenglass, Ethel Rosenberg's brother, whose testimony had doomed her to the chair. Greenglass was so nervous he wouldn't come out of his cell. Even Al despised him for testifying against his sister.

Al had five or six close friends inside. One was a Korean war conscientious objector, practically the only conscientious objector in that war that I've ever heard of. He was a Jewish intellectual whom Al called Clovis, after Clovis Sangrail, the elegant hero of Saki's short stories. He and Al talked art and literature, and Al loaned him old copies of *The New Statesman*, one of the two magazines he was allowed to subscribe to at Lewisburg — the other was *The New Yorker*. Another one of Al's friends was an ethical conman who'd been in the frozen-lobster-tail business in pre-Castro Cuba, a man who said he couldn't con anybody who trusted him, because that was against his principles. When this guy got out he turned to conning old ladies into giving mutts good homes. He'd take a stray, wash it and feed it, and then go to the public library and look up what rare pedigreed breed it most closely resembled. When old ladies later admired the pooch on the street he would reluctantly make them a present of the almost unique specimen.

Al's closest friends were all Italians. Two were young prize fighters, both of them wild kids, one of whom later calmed down and made it big outside the ring, the other of whom never calmed down and ended up dead, dying, as his friends said, like a dog in the rain.

Carmine, another man with whom Al was very thick, was the son of a big-time operator on Long Island who wanted his son to go straight. So he sent Carmine to a fancy prep school, but the kid hated it and kept begging his father to let him go into the business. Finally, the old man, a man of subtle sensibilities, relented. After Carmine's mother died his father fell in love with another woman, but instead of marrying her right away brought her into the house as Aunt So-and-So, someone who had come to help look after Carmine and his sister. Two years later the father told the children he wanted to marry the woman but wouldn't unless they approved of the match. By that time, of course, they'd come to like her, because she was a nice woman, and so when their father did remarry they had no resentment toward their stepmother.

Al got to meet this old gentleman in the visiting room at Lewisburg. Prisoners weren't supposed to talk to anyone but their own families, but Carmine had told his father about Al. So Al would nod at the old gent, and the old gent would nod back from across the room. The visitors' room was the only nice room in Lewisburg, furnished with what looked like wicker patio furniture and always full, whenever I was there, of big Italian families talking loud and laughing and enjoying themselves. When Carmine's old man finally died he willed his son the entire business. Carmine's way of handling Lewisburg was to will himself to go to sleep and stay asleep indefinitely.

I guess Al's two closest friends at Lewisburg were Vincenzo and Angelo, both of whom had been prosecuted by Roy Cohn when he was an assistant United States attorney, both of whom had been promised deals in return for testimony, deals which they turned down. Al discovered that Italians were routinely framed by the federal government — that, in fact, was the only way the feds ever nabbed them. Italians were, and are, for example, routinely locked up on contempt of court charges, for six, eight, and ten months — in one case, for several years, a procedure not envisaged in the U.S. Constitution. Civil libertarians have never protested these incarcerations. Vincenzo was the king of Lewisburg, an important man on the outside whom Al met the first day he was inside because he'd happened to meet the man's brother-in-law at West Street.

Vinnie once saved Al's life. What was important to Vinnie was whether you could do your time like a man and keep your self-respect or just behave like a punk and forget your own humanity. Vinnie, like Al, was already almost a middle-aged man — Al was called "Pop" by all the kids — and Vinnie spent a lot of time talking to the kids to keep them from flying off the handle. One day two kids, not attached to any organization and recently arrived at the joint, went to him for advice. They told him that a guard who had a reputation at Lewisburg for being, as they said, a dog at heart, had said to them, "The Rosenbergs are dead, why should this man Alger Hiss be alive?" The kids asked Vinnie if they should kill Al. Vinnie told them, "This guard can't help you, can't make your life any easier here. Forget it. I know Hiss, he's not so bad." Vinnie then told Al to keep his nose extra-clean for a while. Al managed to get word out to his lawyers, so they would know what had happened if anything ever did happen. The situation blew over, and a couple of months later, the guard, who had been at Guadalcanal, cut his own throat with a razor.

Vinnie also had to calm Al down once, too. Al's lawyers were moving for a new trial and had hired Pearl and Martin Tytell, the best typewriter experts in the business, to build a typewriter just like the old Hiss typewriter in order to demonstrate that forgery by typewriter was a real possibility. The

Tytells made such an exact copy of Woodstock # 230,099 that Miles Lane, the U.S. attorney arguing against the motion, who in court ridiculed their machine as "a Rube Goldberg," subsequently told Pearl Tytell, when she happened to run into him somewhere else, "You people did a phenomenal job; a fantastic job." Al was convinced that this new evidence would spring him immediately and went off to Vinnie and asked him what errands he could run for him on the outside. Vinnie said, "Sit down, Al, and have a cup of coffee." Vinnie was right, of course — old Judge Goddard turned down the motion for a new trial like a shot. The Tytells are still in business — in 1974 they pinpointed the machine Dita Beard had typed her famous memos on. Vinnie also taught Al how to play handball, a game that was new to Al, and wised him up to a number of tricky drop shots you could use to get your opponent to run all over the court without having to do much running around yourself.

Vinnie also got Al to teach Pasquale, one of the prize fighters, how to read and write. Pasquale had beckoned to Vinnie one day in the yard and Vinnie had thought, what kind of trouble is he in now? But Pasquale had said, "I have a letter from my wife." When Vinnie said, "So?" Pasquale said, "Will you read it to me, please? I can't read." Vinnie said, "What are you talking? This is America?" Pasquale said, "I can't read." So Vinnie read the letter and then wrote an answer to Pat's wife. "Dearest Darling, I miss you and the kids very much. I would like to be with you." Vinnie couldn't take too much of this, and he got Al to take on the job. Al says teaching was tough going because the only education books he could get hold of were Dick and Jane books, which Pat hated. One day he found out why Pat had never learned to read. At six or seven he had run home from school one day, and when the truant officers had come to the door he had hid under his mother's bed. His mother, who spoke almost no English, wouldn't tell the truant officers where he was, so they hit her. After that he refused to learn anything in school, but under Al's tutelage he got so he could write home.

Vinnie also tried to reason with Al about being more circumspect in the yard. Prisoners worked from eight in the morning until four in the afternoon every day, and then went out into the yard for exercise. Every day when Al got into the yard there was a line of forty or fifty people with legal papers they wanted him to go over. The prison authorities didn't go for this, because, of course, all these guys wanted Al to help them get out. And Vinnie kept asking Al to cool it, warning him he'd wind up in Atlanta. Al couldn't bring himself to say no. All the inmates who knew Alger called him Al — the first people he had ever met who did that. It was Vinnie who gave Al a new name — Alberto. Vinnie said Alger wasn't a real name.

After a spell in the dormitory, Al was put in the honors wing, the J Wing. He was allowed to receive seven letters or postcards a week and he could write three two-page letters a week. He Scotch-taped the Matisse and Renoir postcards Prossy sent him over his bed. Everyone marveled at how much food he put away every day, because they all hated the prison food. They liked smuggled food better, like the steaks Al occasionally scored from the storeroom and stuffed into his shirt so the guards wouldn't find them.

The inmates were routinely and continually inspected and frisked by the guards — and Al would occasionally not shave as a subtle way of defying the guards' authority. Vinnie occasionally joined Al in this protest, but he thought Al was brave and foolhardy to smuggle steaks and risk getting sent to Atlanta. The only way of cooking these steaks at first was boiling them in the shower, which wasn't very good for them, until Angelo, Al's other closest friend, got a little electric plate from one of his friends in the radio shop. And after that they broiled the steaks while Angie stood at the window waving a towel to get the smell out of the room. Angelo did hard time, that is to say, he hated the joint more than either Al or Vincenzo. But Angie knew how to look after himself: at West Street, the zoo, where no one was treated well, he had managed to get himself assigned to a private room in the infirmary and placed on an ulcer diet, which consisted of real food instead of prison food. He also got a doctor to prescribe a heat lamp for him, and he used the heat lamp to broil steaks. Angie also spent his last months at Lewisburg on the prison farm, outside the walls, an option never offered Al. Angelo's comment on the regular prison food was, they can pattie you to death — meaning that almost the only meat served was meat patties.

Angie liked the farm. "The peaches, Al," he would say, "the tomatoes." Angie made his own peach brandy. He also tried making wine — he'd take the hacks' (the guards') grapes when he went to their houses on the garbage detail and bury bottles of grape juice in the ground. The trouble was he dug them up after a month because he couldn't wait a year, and he could never make anything happen in a month. On the farm Angie got a job checking waterpipes. This was indoor work — he sat in a shanty all day, "where the sun wasn't beating on me," and looked after valves that needed no regulation. One day he and a black guy named Shoes were cooking a chicken in the shanty when they spotted Lieutenant Stafford, a guard, on the way. Angie buried the chicken, although it killed him to do so. Shoes wanted to keep the chicken, but he sprayed some chlorine around the shanty. Stafford said, "What are you cooking?" Angie said, "Cooking? What cooking?" Stafford said, "I smell something."

Angie said, "Maybe what you smell is we threw away some orange rinds and peaches." "No," said Stafford, "it's not fruit. I smell meat." But he couldn't find any, and went away baffled.

A hundred and fifty inmates were detailed to the farm. Angie got there with quite a bit of time left to serve, thanks to the intervention of the Reverend Deitrich, one of the chaplains. The warden called Angie in and said, "Angelo, I can't understand this. This chaplain recommends you so highly." Angie decided to try what he called "a little underground psychology" on the warden. He said, "You don't have to send me out there if you don't want to, warden. You're the boss here." The warden said, "Well, you're right, it's our policy not to send men out there until their time is almost over." Angie said, "Warden, you do what you think is right. I don't want to get you in any trouble." The warden sent him to the farm.

Deitrich would come out to the farm in the boiling sun, wearing a cassock. Then he'd hang up his coat and whisper to Angie, "They're in my coat." The coat was full of cigars. Angie saw him years later in Indiana, where he was the pastor of a nice church. He gave Angie dinner in the rectory and showed him around the church, turning on all the lights. "I can't forget that man," Angie would say. "He was a reverend, but he was a regular person." In Indiana, Deitrich drove around in a bright red sports car, a present from one of his former Lewisburg friends. He would spot new guys coming into the place and tell Angie, "Tell them if I can do anything for them, just let me know." Angie would say, "Take it easy, Reverend, don't worry. I'll take care of it." One of the minister's services was kiting letters, that is, taking uncensored letters in and out, a service every inmate was interested in. The only charge the government could get to stick against Father Philip Berrigan a few years back was that of smuggling a letter out of prison — this was at the same time he was acquitted of charges of conspiring to kidnap Henry Kissinger and blow up tunnels in Washington, charges that had been publicly announced, before any indictment, by J. Edgar Hoover.

Hoover, while we're on the subject, was in Al's mind the principal beneficiary of Al's conviction. He read me a passage from Justice Douglas's autobiography the other day which takes the same view: "The result of the Hiss case was to exalt the informer, who in Anglo-American history has had an odious history. It gave agencies of the federal government unparalleled power over the private lives of citizens. It initiated the regime of sheeplike conformity by intimidating the curiosity and idealism of our youth. It fashioned a powerful political weapon out of vigilantism." Al didn't think much about Dick Nixon, whom he saw as just a solo operator making his way in the world.

Angie and Vinnie, with some assistance from Deitrich, helped make things easier inside for Vinnie's friend, Frank Costello. When Frank arrived at Lewisburg, some of the hillbilly tough guys tried to give him a hard time, saying, "He's just a number like us now." The hillbillies did hard time — they didn't have any commissary, unlike the other inmates, because their families didn't send them any money. If your family sent you some dough, you could spend $10, later upped to $12, a month on cigarettes and candy. The hillbillies in the clothing department gave Frank Costello clothes that wouldn't fit. For handkerchiefs, Frank had to use thin old strips of sheets, and Frank, who was used to the best, couldn't stand that. Angie made sure he got Frank six hand-rolled linen handkerchiefs. When Angie's sister came to visit he would say, "Let me blow my nose." He would pretend to blow his nose on one of her hankies, then put it in his pocket.

Vinnie introduced Al to Costello, and Al decided he was

O.K. when Costello told him the person he admired above all others in modern political life was Eleanor Roosevelt. Costello, too, was in on a bum rap, a contempt charge, and he showed Al the brief his lawyers had written for him. Al said, "Well, they're a good firm. They're my lawyers too." Costello's brief had been written by Bob Benjamin, the lawyer with whom Al had written his own appeals brief. A couple of fairies in the laundry tried to spite Al by cutting one of his pants legs shorter than the other, but he never complained. Sometimes, when Angie would come in from the farm for Sunday church services, he would strap a slice of pheasant breast to his chest for Al. Angie liked to throw rocks at the pheasants. One day a local farm kid outside the fence shot a pheasant, which fell down just inside the fence. Angie leaped on the bird, but the kid pleaded for the bird with tears in his eyes. "I've been out all day. I never shot one before." Angie couldn't take this and said he just had to give it back. "Besides," he added, "the hacks were watching when the kid approached the fence."

The guards on the farm tended to be more relaxed than the guards inside. Sometimes they'd knock on Angie's door after lights out. "Angie, what do you want, a cup of coffee?" "Coffee," he'd say, "I need something more substantial. I drink coffee in the morning." He and a guard would go downstairs and the guard would unlock the big lock on the icebox and they'd have milk and cornflakes and honeybuns. Angie would say, "Can I take a bun for my friend? He couldn't eat today. He's not feeling well." "Don't take too many," the guard would say. "No, of course not," Angie would say, putting four or five in his pocket. Then he'd tell the guard, "I took one."

Sometimes Al would get word, "Angie's coming in today from the farm at two." Angie would be going on sick call — "I had so many toothaches in those days," he would say later.

So Al would go on sick call too, and they'd have time to chat. Angie said, "It was rough here in the beginning, Al, but then we got the place set up." Angie's other main connection was the hack around the barbershop where Angie worked for a while. He took his work seriously. "I didn't have to cut no hair, only my friends. I'm not a barber, Al, I'm a hair stylist. I mean if you can't style hair, you'll never make it." When Angie went to court to be sentenced, the city marshal who accompanied him happened to be someone he'd known from his old neighborhood. The man put the cuffs so loose on Angie's wrists that Angie slipped them off. His mind raced. Should he make a break for it? But he figured he still might beat the rap. The judge sentencing him said, "Ten years on possession, ten years on selling, five years on conspiracy . . . to be served concurrently." "Thank God he said concurrently, Al, and not consecutively. With one word he could have killed me." Angie went straight after getting out. He took a job in Jersey. He liked to dress nice, and he used to appreciate it when Al would go and visit him. "Al," he would say, "your tie," and he would straighten Al's tie. A couple of years ago at Christmas time, Al took him a bottle of Scotch, Cutty Sark, his favorite brand. Angie opened the box with the Christmas gift wrapping on it. Then he looked hurt. "Al," he said, "no card?"

A dramatic moment inside for Al came on sundown, June 19, 1953, the day the Rosenbergs were executed. At West Street Al had met Morton Sobell, convicted at the same time as the Rosenbergs for conspiring to steal atomic secrets for the Russians. Sobell, who was going off to Alcatraz to do thirty years, told Al the whole case had been a frame. "The night they died, that was quite an evening," Al says. It was the only time while he was there that there was an attitude of sullen bitterness throughout the entire prison. "The solemnness, the brooding, the bitterness, it was extremely dramatic. Of course, they weren't executed at Lewisburg. That didn't matter, it was just as though you were in a pen where someone was going to be executed. We'd heard some pharisaical business about how they couldn't be executed during the day because it was the Sabbath, and that they were going to be electrocuted when the sun set. Nobody had any political interest in the Rosenbergs, but it was their idea that you don't execute women. At sundown that day there was a mood that would be . . . ah . . . very hard to describe. Except to say absolute silence. Handball games stopped, everything. People sat tensely, solemnly, angrily, while they knew this was going on."

Al also met a couple of Communist leaders who had been convicted just about the same time he was, under a Smith Act charge of conspiring to overthrow the government. He didn't talk to them much, and he never talked politics with them. A number of the prisoners observing this said that that convinced them of Al's innocence. Vincenzo's opinion was "Alberto is a man. If he wanted to be a Communist, he has every right to be a Communist, because a man can believe anything he wants to. I can believe anything I want to, as long as I don't try to make you believe the same thing. But Alberto has never once said anything to me on the subject, except that he was innocent, and I know him, and he's not the kind of man who if he believes something would pretend he didn't. I know people. In nineteen thirty-two, in the middle of the depression, when I was twenty-one years old, I was running the numbers in three different Pennsylvania cities and making a thousand a week. You have to know people to run a business like that. And I know that Alger Hiss is no Communist."

When Al got out of jail, he was asked by the American Friends Service Committee if he wanted to participate in their efforts at prison reform. He said, no, he didn't, because he didn't think prisons were going to change until society changes. Al got out of stir on November 27, 1954, two weeks and two days after his fiftieth birthday. When he walked out the main gate other inmates jammed the windows and cheered and applauded.

7. Son of Liar

W HEN I WAS a kid — I was born August 5, 1941 — I revered Al, but I didn't see very much of him because he wasn't home a hell of a lot, and I wasn't sure he liked me, because aside from spanking me once when I crept downstairs in Washington one night while he and mom were having a party he didn't take too much of a hand in bringing me up. He tells me I was a happy baby who liked traveling and didn't cry much — I don't remember. People who visited the house when I was tiny say mom, instead of stopping me when I did something she didn't want me to, engaged me in discussions of the pros and cons — I don't remember. Others say she spoiled me rotten. That Al would get mad at the way she indulged me but would react by taking a walk around the block. I don't know about that — my first conscious memories are of falling out of a baby carriage and smashing my two front teeth and of sitting with my baby sitter, Mrs. Greene, in the empty front upstairs room of the house we moved into when I was three watching guys haul furniture into the house.

I remember vividly the day Roosevelt died — I mean I remember that something terrible had happened because mom and dad were both shocked, and moved around the house like they'd been drugged. Presidential elections got to me for quite a while after that — the morning after the '48 election when no one was sure yet who had won I ran out of school assembly — we were in New York by this time — in tears because someone said Dewey had beaten Truman. Election night '52 it was just mom and me and my second-grade teacher, Louise Carpenter — Al was 19137 — eating hamburgers at Hamburg Heaven just before Ike won like it was the last meal in Paris before the Panzers arrived. I don't remember 1956 at all, so it wore off and anyway by then I was interested in the New York Giants.

My other Washington memories — we moved to New York when I was six — add up to this: there was a nice red rug on the dining room floor and I liked to march around the table on it, but I didn't know Whittaker Chambers had given it to Al; the gingko trees smelled; my cousin Bosley, Donie's kid, was bad, once peeing in the wading pool. Another time he climbed off a seesaw and I bumped down on the other end on my back and was pretty sure that it was broken and my legs with any luck would be paralyzed like President Roosevelt's and Al would be my friend. Al had an astonishing number of suits and shoes and shoetrees and ties and he always wore a white handkerchief in the breast pocket of his jacket and looked like a million; I once saw my brother wearing a sailor suit; Al at bedtime told me the story of the White Rabbit who looked at his watch and said, "Oh dear, oh dear, I shall be late"; Prossy at bedtime would put her hands together and circle them over my stomach and say, "Once upon a time there was an eagle named George *Washington*." When she got to *Washington* her hands pounced on my tum.

One night Al and Prossy got dressed up to go somewhere, leaving me with Mrs. Greene, but returned unexpectedly with a kitten they'd found on the street, because they couldn't stand seeing the kitten look lonely. This kitten grew up to be a very cranky cat named Putter and was my best friend and the only person I didn't have any doubts about until she died my first year in high school. We'd had an aged dog before that, a cocker spaniel named Jenny — originally the puppy Al had bought for Tim — but I really remember only how marvelously she behaved toward me. Supposedly she had all kinds of ulcers or sores on her stomach but wouldn't complain when I manhandled her.

According to my nursery school report card for June 1945, when I was three going on four, "Tony is not completely relaxed physically . . . seems to enjoy the stimulus offered by puzzles, if he does not lose patience . . . tends to substitute fussiness & whining for language when frustrated or when he can't get his own way . . . loves stories . . . Tony's vocabulary is exceptional for his age. He enunciates well, speaks distinctly, uses good grammar and sentence structure. We feel that he is somewhat dependent on language for security — he repeats questions, and 'why,' and expects attention from others during play when he verbalizes. He enjoys talking, and is experimenting with imitative, random sounds and at present with verbal negativism. This developmental negativism usually appears earlier and wears itself out eventually. Routines are easier for him, but *will* stimulate it, as do other situations, i.e. riding in Mrs. W.'s car. In such cases as this, we feel Tony should be helped in making a decision, and standing by it." That sounds like me, all right.

Alger and Prossy — I called them that from quite an early age — sent postcards when they were out of town. A big one of Old North Church, Boston, from Al to Master Anthony Hiss, dated December 5, 1944, says: "Dear Tony, Did you ever see such a big postal card? I never did before. I know you like steeples and horses. This picture has both, so

I hope you will like it. I expect that you and Mrs. Greene are having a good time. Much love, Alger." A letter from mom the following summer from Peacham, Vermont: "Dearest Tony Darling, How sorry I was to hear you were sick. If Dr. Nicholson says you have Mumps, cheer up because both Paul and Johnny Hoff have had them and you can play with them anyway. We are having a nice rest in the country. This morning I heard a crow saying: CAW, CAW, CAW, CAW, CAW, CAW. Six times! Now what do you think he was trying to say? Much much love from Prossy."

I liked Peacham a lot — an eighteenth-century village in the hills of northeastern Vermont where Harvard professors summered. The Congregational church had a bell in the steeple that had maybe been cast by Paul Revere, you could still see where the beaver hat factory had stood at the turn of the century, and the Peacham Academy — the town high school — had been in business since 1797. Al hung out with John Varnum, a guy who made butter molds and fixed things, the only Democrat ever elected to the state legislature from Caledonia County. John once fixed a lady's coffee pot, and when she said, "How much do I owe ya?" and he said, "A nickel," she slowly pulled out her purse and said, "Well, I'd rather overpay you than not pay you at all."

I liked Eddie Allen, the only taxi driver in the county, and Crazy Ned, who ate Hershey bars in church, and Howard Hebblethwaite's combination ice-cream-parlor-and-lending-library where I read Uncle Wiggily stories, as soon as I could read. Population: a couple hundred. Everyone was related to everyone, naturally, and it turned out mom was related to them, too, if you cut just a couple of corners. The phones were wooden wall phones you had to crank, and when one day Dar-Dar, one of the old-time summer folk, said, on the phone, "I wish Mrs. Hobart wouldn't listen to all the conversations," she was accosted the next day at the general store by Mrs. Hobart, the telephone operator, who said, "I do *not* listen in on people's conversations." The town was serviced by a small, independent phone company, the Mollies Falls Telephone Company, and a call to a town five miles away on the Bell system had to go over fifteen miles of Mollies Falls wires. I guess it's obvious I liked the place — lazy summers outdoors, a housekeeper named Aunt Rena Hunter, who kept mom off my neck, bare feet, Harvey's Pond to swim in, Flippie Craig from up the hill to play with, and the Bungess girls, and a nice girl named Missy who stayed in our house a couple of summers.

I read under the covers with a flashlight, and in September went to the local one-room schoolhouse for a month with the other kids because Dalton started late. This always gave me a jump on the school year because Dalton used the same books the Vermont schools did. One September the fad for lunch was cold corn on the cob. When Al and Prossy woke up Aunt Rena once in the middle of the night to look at an eclipse of the moon, she took one look, said, "What next?" and went back to bed. When Prossy baked her first apple pie, Aunt Rena said, "You'll excuse me, Mrs. Hiss, but my teeth cost me a hundred dollars, so I won't eat the bottom crust."

At the Peacham school baseball games I always wanted to be umpire, a position that seemed to offer power but didn't demand coordination, but at Dalton I tried not to be a sissy and eventually scored four points in the final basketball game of eighth grade, my last year, a career high. Dalton at that time seemed to go in for celebrities' grandchildren more than anything else. Bobby Fisk, in my class, was Averill Harriman's grandson, and Carol Isaacs was the granddaughter of Stanley Isaacs, who was known as the Conscience of the City Council. The brightest kids in the class were Jews — I played three-dimensional tick tack toe in math class with Bill Harris and became a "unit hound" with him and Chris Schwabacher, whose mother took us to the circus every year. Unit hound refers to The Dalton Plan, which was an idea that children should study subjects by the month. So each month was divided into twenty units of work, and we all had unit cards, and when you finished an assignment you filled in the units in black, and when the teachers okayed the work they marked that in red. And we fought to see who could get his card filled up first and signed by the teachers — "get off his assignment" was the phrase — because as soon as you were off your assignment you could tack the unit card up on the wall of your homeroom. There was usually a photo finish. After we got bored getting off our assignments, which was pretty easy, we fought to see who could get the most "EXC"s, "V.G."s and "GOOD"s on a unit card — Johnny Seeger, Pete Seeger's brother, our geography teacher, was always a soft touch for an "EXC." because he was always good-natured except once a month when he blew up and yelled, "I cannot stand so much noise in this classroom," which could be heard all over the seventh floor.

In seventh grade, at the age of twelve, I would stay up until after midnight to make sure my homework was perfect. Dalton was on East 89th Street, between Park and Lexington, and most of the kids lived around there. There were two black kids in the class, one of them the son of a lady judge, and one Chinese boy, Henry Lee. My best friend was George Engel, quarterback of the football team, who won every election. I always came in second. I edited two blackboard newspapers, "The Family Eagle" and "The Seventh Floor News." George edited "The Family Beagle," which later changed its name to "Sports Un-Illustrated," and occasionally Roger Barzun, Jacques Barzun's son, edited "The Barzun Bugle." They were all written on a blackboard with chalk. George's father had run a famous upper Madison Avenue dress shop that went under when too many of its customers started taking dresses, wearing them to a party, and then returning them for credit the next morning.

During the Hiss case I lived one year at the Buttenwiesers' — 17 East 73rd. That was a town house with a private elevator and Chris Schwabacher and I would spend hours riding up and down. The Buttenwiesers made me feel at home and I began to equate "rich" with "nice." Al says I told him once, "The Buttenwiesers are very rich." "How do you know?" "They have lamb chops all the time." Prossy's menus, although her nickname for me was "Lambchop," ran heavily to starches, potato casseroles with cheese and bacon bit topping, and the like. Except the year she read Adelle Davis and started putting eggshells in things. Or wheat germ or kale. The one piece of advice Helen Buttenwieser gave me in those days — she had been a Lehman — was "If someone asks you the time on the street, don't tell them. They want your watch." The one piece of advice Prossy gave me at the time was "If someone takes you out to dinner at a restaurant, always look at the right-hand side of the menu first." Schwabacher tells me — I had forgotten this — that when I lived at the Buttenwiesers' I had a three-foot schmoo with a beanbag in it (so it would bounce up when you hit it) that I called "Nixon." I liked to punch it and jump on it. At Halloween I sent Al and Prossy a card that said "A PUMPKIN PAPER PLANTED BY ME (BOO)." When you opened it up it said "This Pumpkin Paper asks Mr. and Mrs. Alger Hiss to have a HAPPY HALOWEEN. Tony (signature forged)."

After the Hiss case I lived with Prossy and Putter on 8th Street. One Sunday we went to brunch at the Buttenwiesers' and when it came time to go I wouldn't leave. In fact, I went limp and collapsed in their front hall. Prossy was mad, and Helen, who was embarrassed, tried to push me out the door. At which point I said, "Kicking a man out of his own house!" When Al went off to jail Prossy at first considered spending

winters in an unheated house in Peacham, where the tempera-
ture gets down to around forty below, or finding a remote
cottage on the Eastern Shore. She also thought of entering
domestic service, but in the end she took a job in the base-
ment of a Doubleday Book Shop, underneath Fifth Avenue,
for the take-home pay of thirty-seven dollars a week. She told
Al, when we went down to Lewisburg to visit him, that all
their old friends had abandoned her. He found this hard to
believe. She did make some new friends at Doubleday, but
when Al came back and they met him and liked him, too, she
dropped them. She didn't have any boyfriends.

She also got pneumonia once, and Tim, who was living in
New York then and dropped in occasionally — he had decided to become a doctor and was putting himself through
premed at NYU by working night shifts as an orderly at
Bellevue, hired a private nurse whom Prossy didn't like.
Tim later went to medical school in Switzerland and immediately after that moved to California and never again
moved back east. Her memory of these years, as she told John
Smith last year, is that she was "carrying the flag for the
family." She used to tell me, especially around Christmas,
that "the family is still together because you and I are still
here." She also used to tell me to be "bonny," which meant
to be cheerful outside of the house or in front of company.
She didn't buy new clothes or spend much on food, but she
did pay for piano lessons for me and kept her subscription to
the New York Philharmonic — two balcony seats on odd
Thurdays.

What I remember is the trip down to see Al was not supposed to be fun; the house got cluttered with newspapers and
magazines on chairs and tables; I ate a lot of burnt toast and
burnt oatmeal; she started to get fat; I started to get fat; I
started staying up late every night sweating over my homework; I found it impossible one spring to decide whether to

go to camp that summer in Montana or Vermont or go to Peacham or stay in New York; I read books whenever I didn't have to do anything else — my favorites were about Freddy the Pig, a talking pig on a farm in Upstate New York who edited a newspaper and whose best friend was a cat; our apartment smelled of cat piss in the winter because the cat pan was next to a radiator and the cat peed on the radiator pipe which volatilized it effectively; I dragged my feet whenever it was time to go home from school or whenever Prossy told me to do anything. I was angry at Al for leaving me to live with a lot of men, and I also felt that Prossy was somehow stronger than Al, because she was still there and he wasn't.

I started seeing a shrink a couple times a week. Lou Gilbert was an ortho-Sullivanian, a nice guy who gave me ginger ale and Scottish oatcakes. We built model railroad stations together while I told him about wanting to jump off the balcony of Carnegie Hall and about dreams that teachers would reject my homework and the recurring dream he called the "Arietty dream," which was based on a children's book about a tiny family that live behind the walls of a big family's house and are menaced by cats but befriended by the daughter of the big family, Arietty. Only in my dream I was one of the little people and the cat was no threat but Arietty wanted to squeeze me. When Chester Lane, the lawyer, drove Prossy and me down to Lewisburg to pick up Al the day he was released, Prossy kept pounding Chester on the shoulder while he was driving calmly and saying, "Keep calm, Chester! Keep calm!"

Al sent me off to the Putney School in Vermont for high school, so I wasn't around much during the years when he and Prossy started fighting — he walked out on her in January 1959, the day I went back to school for winter term my senior year. He'd told me the previous fall, at the Putney

Harvest Festival, that the marriage was pfft but that he wouldn't leave until I left for school after Christmas. The previous summer, when things were thunderous between Al and Prossy, the three of us had driven up to Canada, and I would talk to first one and then the other privately and ask them to be nice to each other, just like I was a little United Nations. Putney was a co-ed prep school, two hundred kids on an old farm nestled in the foothills of Vermont. The history teacher the fall of my freshman year was named Dr. Lee Su Yan, and he taught history by rote. We were all expected to memorize a long chart of world history — "History is man's story — is *his story*, see? I want you to write everything in yink, my boy. Sit down, and don't move your chair or I have to count off your mark." The chart commenced: "Peking man — 500,000 B.C. Java Man — 400,000 B.C." Dr. Lee left suddenly three days before Christmas vacation. We heard later that he had gone to Seattle, where he had been picked up on some charge by the Feds. After that we learned that he had originally been hired by the school as a cook but when there was a vacancy in the history department he had produced credentials from a Chinese university. Finally the mother of my best friend, Jeremy Siepmann, discovered that the Chinese university in question was a two-thousand-year-old ruin.

The school liked to think of itself as an oasis of calm in a troubled time, and there was a lot of talk about the Putney Spirit, which meant not sneaking off into the woods to smoke cigarettes illegally. Anyone who smoked cigarettes illegally was known as a Cynic. The school told me I was on full scholarship — years later I found out that the money had come from Aggie Lockwood, who used to work at the Carnegie Endowment, and her husband. Officially the school had no marks — that meant that you weren't told your grades unless you got either an F or a "3 in effort," but of course transcripts were sent off to colleges. The school had a good music teacher and an excellent Latin teacher, Felix Lederer. The girls never wore make-up. I had a crush on several but never passed beyond the furtive smooching stage. There were lots of hikes, which I enjoyed taking in sport jacket and tie. One winter term, when everyone else was on skis, I managed my schedule so I only had to attend one regularly scheduled sports activity. Actually, the final time I ever did have to ski, in 1959, I sort of enjoyed it, but not enough to ever do it again. My marks were good until Al told me he was leaving home, after which I didn't study much. But that was all right because I'd already gotten into Harvard — where I hardly studied at all. Al wanted me to go to Berkeley — he said Harvard had passed its prime. I thought he was loony. At Putney I continued to come in second in elections. Ditto at Harvard — where I lost a three-way election for president of the Signet Society, the undergraduate literati hangout, between me, David Rockefeller's son, and Garry Moore's son.

At Harvard I started getting up after lunch. I failed two courses — Zeph Stewart's Greek A (he's the brother of Supreme Court justice Potter Stewart) and Howard Mumford Jones's farewell English course (Howard used to summer in Peacham). I was never on probation but only because a series of tutors liked me — first Elliott Perkins, Master of Lowell House, who told me that talking to Nathan Pusey, Harvard president, was like "shootin' bullets in a bag of sand," next Peter Stansky, now a professor at Stanford and who senior year was kind enough to read chapters of my honors thesis on the British General Strike of 1926 — I was majoring in English history and literature — at one and two in the morning. I decided to write a thesis three weeks before it was due, so I did two weeks' research and wrote for a week, on Dexamyl. I larded the thesis with footnotes from Burke's Peerage. Professor H. Stuart Hughes gave me high marks for this, praising the "Veblenesque Irony" of the footnotes, but a graduate student reader marked me down for padding.

I spent most of my time at Harvard at the *Harvard Crimson*, the undergraduate daily paper, which turned out to be smart, because the *Crimson* is the only trade-school experience at Harvard. With a Harvard B.A. (mine came in '63) and a couple of years on the *Crime* you can get out and get a job. I got one writing for The Talk of the Town section of *The New Yorker*, something I still do. The editor of *The New Yorker* knew who I was — his older boy had been two years behind me at Dalton, Putney, and Harvard. I got elected to the *Crimson* the fall of my sophomore year after finding out that the paper's music critic didn't care if he never heard another note in his life. He was about to quit and nobody else wanted the job. I figured I'd picked up enough about music at Putney to fake it and that if during my competition I refused to write anything but music reviews the editors wouldn't be able to find a reason not to elect me. The strategy worked, and a year later, when I didn't care if I never heard another note of music in my life, I elected someone to take my place and began writing savage theater reviews and other feature material. I'd forgotten I could do this musical stuff so well until I saw a piece of mine recently quoted in Richard Bissell's *You Can Always Tell a Harvard Man*: "The first desk winds handled the fugal introduction to the psalm with ease, a particularly delicate passage full of grace and restraint, and in the more monolithic third psalm the brasses showed strength and carefully controlled enthusiasm." "Mr. Hiss," said Bissell, "has got the musical lingo down better than the *Times*." The spring of my senior year I fell in love with a girl who's now a member of the Harvard Board of Overseers. This time I once got as far as petting and felt very grown up.

After college I moved back to Prossy's apartment, because she told me she wanted me there. She was in a bad way at this point — she paced the floor and moaned a lot. She alternated between cursing Al for leaving and making plans for what she'd do after he came back. She also swept one or two rugs for hours because her psychiatrist, a courtly old man named John A. P. Millet, told her she was doing as well as could be expected under the circumstances and that doing housework was good therapy. During this period I spent a a lot of time in the bathtub and learned how to put myself to sleep at will and stay there until it was imperative to go to the bathroom. I would see Al every week or two for lunch, and I was usually half to three quarters of an hour late and picked fights with him and was rude to his friends. I was jealous of his not being at 8th Street and I was also still operating under the assumption that Prossy held the reins of power.

Of course, I wasn't the only one operating under that assumption. Tim, a couple of years after Al moved out on Prossy, wrote him a letter from San Francisco where he was an intern, telling Al to give Prossy whatever she wanted, including plenty of money, to satisfy any whims or necessities she might have; that it was necessary to support her anxieties rather than confront them.

A couple of years after I started working at *The New Yorker* and went back to living with Prossy, I finally got into bed with a girl for the first time and couldn't get it up, even though I'd had a hard-on while talking her into it. My first thought was that I ought to propose marriage to her, since we'd slept together, and my second thought was, since I hadn't been able to fuck her, I must be a fairy. I told Al I thought I was a fairy, and he said, "I thought this was coming. Now I can tell you that your brother thought he was one, too." My Harvard roommate told me he hadn't been able to get it up the first time he'd slept with a girl, either, but I thought I was still doomed. So I decided to get a boyfriend. I found one who hated me, which seemed to me only right, and hung around him for a while.

But in the meantime, I moved out on Prossy, realizing, finally, that it hadn't killed Al to do so. I didn't exactly leave the neighborhood, but I went first to an apartment on Waverly Place which I shared with a couple of guys, and then to my own place on West 10th Street, and for some reason my life started to change. I started working at my job, instead of seeing how many weeks I could sleep through not picking up my paychecks; I started meeting lots of people who enjoyed their lives; I met a nice girl and was able to fuck her; I got to be good friends with Al, even showing up on time when we had lunch; I founded *The Real World* magazine with my friend Stephen Shore, the photographer; I traveled; I bought new clothes and wore aviator glasses instead of hornrims; I started going to a good barber; I wrote a book with my friend E. M. Frimbo, the world's greatest railroad buff; I grew a mustache; I started growing roses on West 10th Street. Things like that. These things took a few years — something like five or six — to happen but they all happened. Last year I even got a driver's license — to me a miracle. So what changed my life? Well, part of it was I finally started to get to know my dad, and he turned out to be Al rather than anybody else. But the main thing was just realizing what most people get around to realizing sooner or later. I'm alive, and I can do things, so what else is there to do but live and do things? Because you never know how long you've got to enjoy it. Which is true whether your father is Dick Nixon, Whit Chambers, Al Hiss, or any man or Disco Duck.

Six months ago I decided to do something I'd wanted to do for a long time, I don't know why, something it seemed to me no one in the family would ever do — be a bartender. I'd never had to work standing up, or serve people, or even talk to them on the job without a notebook in my hand. A friend of mine,

Steve Resnick, who owns a friendly bar and restaurant with a working fireplace on West 72nd Street in New York called the All State Café, agreed after he'd satisfied himself that I didn't want to do this just to write about it, to let me train under a couple of his bartenders. One of these guys, an old pro my age named Mike Slater, told me later he will never forget the pain it caused him to watch me mix my first martini: the hesitation, the agonizing slowness, the pitiful helplessness, the fear and shaking of limbs. But thanks to Slater and his colleague, John Lafayette, I picked up the basics of the trade after a while, mostly because they were both good teachers. Meaning they were kind enough to stick me behind the bar and then sit in a corner and not rush to my assistance even when all the deftness in them screamed out for them to rush over and grab a bottle out of my less than prehensile grasp. After I'd been up to the bar a few times I told Al, a bit diffidently, that I was opening up a new sideline. He didn't say much about that or react one way or another. What was the bastard thinking? Al can still play it close to the chest when he feels like it. A couple of months later I told him Resnick had just told me I was ready for my first solo on the "graveyard shift," the Saturday daytime hitch — generally a small crowd and mainly brunch, beer, and bloody marys. Al said, "Well, now you've done everything I always wanted to do. When I was just out of college I wanted to be a bartender; I've always enjoyed pouring drinks for friends. I guess the one thing I wanted to do you haven't done is learn how to play the French horn."

8. A Good Life Is
the Best Revenge

WHEN AL GOT BACK from Lewisburg, Prossy suggested that the two of them run away and change their names and hide off in some small school somewhere. Al didn't take this very seriously but he was riled when his parole officer suggested the same thing. For sixteen months after he left prison he wasn't allowed to travel more than fifty miles outside of New York and had to report to a parole officer once a week. "Change your name," said the parole officer. "Then you won't have to live this thing down." "I had thought I got along very well with my parole officer," Al said. He didn't look for work because all the time he'd been inside he'd wanted to write a book about the Hiss case. But the authorities hadn't let him. So he got an agent, who got him $5000 advances from two publishers. And the three Hisses lived on the ten grand for a year.

But Al didn't start writing the book for a few months because he was having a good time. "The world was new and fresh all over again." Prossy was off all day at Doubleday's and Al started going to the art museums and taking walks in Central Park with a woman who'd been a very famous actress in Austria before the war and whom Al had met at Vi

Bernard's house during the trials. She said, "Look, we're acting like a couple of adolescents!" Al found her attractive, but he was a married man, so he didn't fool around. "I was so glad to be out of the clink! Prossy got more and more jealous, and I found this more and more annoying, so I broke it off. I was trying to make a go of the marriage and I believed in loyalty, and that was more important to me. So I told Prossy 'If you don't want me to see her, I won't see her.'"

So it was back to the book, published as *In the Court of Public Opinion*. Al says, "I didn't want to go into personal stuff. This was a legal brief — a chance to present the whole case in one place, something I could use my legal talents on" — as a convicted felon Al had automatically been disbarred. "I knew nobody else would write the book — Chester Lane and Bob Benjamin both said they would but they were both too busy."

Did Al enjoy writing? "No, it's too agonizing. I'd just as soon do income tax, although I must say when I got absorbed, it went quickly. But I would sharpen pencils by the hour and walk up and down. It didn't take as long as I'd expected — I got the damn thing done by the fall of fifty-five." Knopf smelled best-seller and printed 60,000 copies, but the book didn't catch on, unlike Whit Chambers' Book-of-the-Month Club selection *Witness*, which netted him half a million. Reviewers objected to Al's style, saying it had no emotion, but the point is it only has one emotion: These things can't happen but they happened. Chambers' book, like all his stories, has emotions like Abbott had Costello — "Time-Life Dostoievski," is the way I. F. Stone puts it.

In April 1956 Al made his first post-Lewisburg public appearance, addressing the Whig-Clio debating club at Princeton. Alumni gifts failed to drop the next year (they rose), but a congressman suggested Princeton establish a "Department of Treachery." Somewhere during this period Al had a gall bladder operation, and when he was done with the book he got a job. First he almost got a job. A man who ran an outfit called American Artists Group — it represented, initially, blacklisted artists and later added artists not accused of anything — offered Al a niche as his executive assistant, if Al could learn shorthand and typing. Al enrolled at Speedwriting Institute, the steno school that teaches a shorthand based on the ABCs — they advertise in the New York subways: "f u cn rd th msj u cn gt a gd jb + mo pa." The lady who ran the school liked him so much she gave him a full scholarship. Al mastered Speedwriting. "But in a crisis I always reverted to my own shorthand that I developed in law school. I could keep up with the dictation, but they said it wasn't right. I could not learn to type. I would lie in bed and see the keys perfectly, and I could type with my fingers on the counterpane, but by the time I got to the machine, whenever I hit the space bar, my fingers got out of position and I typed in unknown languages. My teacher gave me special sessions. She said, 'You've got a block about typing — maybe because of that damn case.' I said, 'Maybe you're right.'"

Al missed out on that job — but then he got a solid offer. "I got my job through the New York Times," he says. Peter Kihss, the man known around the Times as the best reporter in the business, happened to write a little follow-up story about the notorious Al and quoted him as saying he was, "looking for work, cheap." Enter Andy Smith, inventor of Feathercombs. Andy and a 4-F pal spent World War II in an advertising agency trying to figure a way to make a million bucks after being rejected by the navy. Calling on his knowledge of Japanese culture — Andy's dad was a missionary — Andy remembered that Japanese women wore a particular kind of fine hair comb made of sprung wire that had enough tension to hold hair better than a bobby pin. So after the war, he imported Swedish piano wire into Japan, where it was

182 / *Laughing Last*

made cheap into Feathercombs, which he then imported into the States, where black and Puerto Rican women on Park Avenue South pasted rhinestones on them. They were put on jobber racks in supermarkets and drugstores and demonstrated at Macy's and Bloomingdale's, and were very popular, particularly after Andy coined the slogan "Fabulous Feathercombs."

Al worked for Feathercombs for two years, '57 and '58. The first year business was good, the second year business was bad. Andy hired him as office manager at $6000 a year, after Al told him he couldn't work for less than $100 a week. "That's one of the reasons I hired you," Andy said later. "I knew you were making $20,000 at the Carnegie Endowment, and I knew I could get you cheap." "Andy was a smart cookie," says Al.

Where Andy went wrong was holding out too long. He turned down a big offer from Gillette for the business. Then Solo tried to buy him and when he wouldn't sell marketed a plastic look-alike and undersold Andy's product. Al brought in Chester Lane's partner, Wally Beer, as general counsel. "It was a very respectable outfit under my direction, for a while," says Al. "I got a first-class patent attorney I'd known in the RCA case, and we won in the lower court, but the legal delays were killing us, because Andy didn't have enough diversification. It was hectic — the hours! I worked like a devil to keep it together. Congressmen used to ask us New Dealers, 'Have you ever met a payroll?' Here I really was meeting a payroll — week to *week*, I had to scrounge around to get the cash. Then we lost an appeal — patents are awfully tricky — and Andy was ruined. He tried to negotiate with Solo, but what they offered at that point was, of course, ridiculous."

Al told Andy he wanted to leave in six months. He also told Andy he should spend more time at the office working on schemes to sell the business and less time in his Porsche, adding, "You are running this job like a love affair." A bad turn of phrase by Al, who says, "I didn't know — everyone else did — that he was having an affair with the chief demonstrator, who was the queen of the hive around there. A coolness set in after that remark. Then I made the great mistake of calling him a liar. You should never call anyone a liar! In front of the staff he told me I shouldn't have done something. I said, 'You told me to!' He said, 'Not at all,' and that's when I said, 'Andy, you're a liar.' From then on I was all washed up, and I had my first heart attack on a train that night on the way to Connecticut. The last couple of months we were factored. I must say I always found the factors to be men of their word."

Al's other heart attack was nothing of the sort, but he still likes to call it that, because that's what he actually thought it was at the time. He was invited to a house party without realizing a pushy woman who drove him up the wall was a fellow guest. "I felt trapped. Growing up in a house full of women, the only kind of women I like are either innocent or direct. This woman supported all the right causes for all the wrong reasons, a hypocrite. She wouldn't let up. I was furious. I got up at six to get out of the house, couldn't find any place open for breakfast, walked miles, got hotter and hotter, and when I got back to the house I had a heart attack, and my host arranged for me to be met by an ambulance — I said I wanted to see my own doctor in town — and I had a compartment all to myself on the train. When I got to New York, my doctor wasn't available, so I went to bed. The next morning I felt fine. Dr. Rubenfine explained it later."

Meanwhile Al and Prossy were fighting, and I was at Putney, so I didn't catch much of it. What I remember is she got hotter and hotter and he got colder and colder. It boiled down to emotion versus intellect, and in the summer of '58

Prossy told him, on the advice, as he later learned, of Dr. Millet, to get out, and threw her wedding ring (platinum) at him. He gave it back to her, saying it was hers no matter what she thought about him, and she kept it and wears it to this day. He told her he wasn't leaving until after my Christmas vacation and started sleeping in the living room. He immediately called up his actress friend, who was vacationing on Mount Desert Island, and when she got back to town they had "a very pleasant winter affair" until Jimmie Byrnes wrote an article about Yalta in either *Life* or *Look* that mentioned Al — "not altogether fondly. My name was again a hot potato, and she said that I was too disturbing, and that I was 'too bossy and upsetting' and broke it off, although I would have been glad to see more of her. She was very cultivated and widely read and knew all the classical drama thoroughly and all that fall while we were together she had a very good part in a play at the old Circle in the Square — I saw that play twenty-five times, and then I'd go backstage, and they had the rattiest dressing rooms. A terrible hell hole."

Al was on unemployment for a year in '59 and got to be good friends with Jack Gilford, who was also standing in the unemployment line for people whose names began with G or H. He slept late every day for some months and didn't shave often after leaving Prossy but then he went down to Texas to visit Anna, and suddenly realized he felt fine. He wrote me a letter at Putney:

"Dear Tones, This is one of the last letters I'll be able to send you for a long time — so I'm trying to protect my average by a lot of letters in these last few weeks. (I'm assuming your European schedule won't be sufficiently fixed for you to be able to get mail this summer.)

"Did you know that on April 16 the *Times* editorial after Foster Dulles's death said J.F.D. had 'sought without deviation a new birth of freedom under God — and this in the true Lincolnian sense . . .'? *Life's* coverage of the funeral was no more feverish: 'A Fighter for the Right, a mighty pillar of the republic.'

"We spent all day today on the campus — a sizeable one (there are over 17,000 students). Anna knows everyone. The Chief of University Police — much more than the typical campus cop, apparently the head of a section of the city police with 50 or 60 men under him equipped with prowl cars, motorcycles, etc. — hailed me because he recognized me as 'looking like Miss Hiss.' . . .

"We went through the Physical Ed. building which is a beauty and met the staff. In the latter part of the afternoon we were with a member of the engineering faculty who is also in charge of administration (architect for new buildings, maintenance and renovation, sculpture, grounds and greenhouses and the campus cops). He told us of one of the older unmarried Klebergs (of the King Ranch) who was at last forced by his relatives to install a water closet. He agreed on one condition, that none of his collections of Texiana be disturbed. They were all over his old ranch house so the toilet had to be installed on the second floor front porch.

"Anna has rented a Rambler for my stay — they are slick little cars, I must say.

"If you get too many of these Texas Rotarian Booster letters send me a wire saying: Stop: for Heaven's sake stop.

"Really, I'm having a ball.
                    "Much love, Alger."

In 1960 Al got a new job and a new girlfriend, the woman he now lives with, a tall good-looking blonde — she looks like Arletty but is otherwise thoroughly American. They've never gotten married, since Prossy still won't give Al a divorce. For a while he pushed for one. Now he doesn't care. He made Prossy get a lawyer by threatening to get a Mexican divorce, but Helen Buttenwicser, representing Al, could never reach any settlement with the guy. He finally called her up and said, "I just discovered my client doesn't *want* a divorce." A year later Helen ran into Prossy on the street and bought a drink and asked her why she didn't want a divorce. Prossy said this, that, and the other thing. Helen asked her, "Are you trying to tell me you want to go down in history as Mrs. Alger Hiss?" Prossy didn't say yes or no, but the card over her doorbell still says "Mrs. Alger Hiss."

The last time Al saw her was a couple of years ago when he ran into her on the street. For a while he took to calling her "Priscilla" or "your mother" when discussing her with me. Now, when he does mention her, it's "Prossy." "I think," he says, "she's always known, as I did, that this nightmare would get straightened out — and she would then be Mrs. Alger Hiss with status again. Let me give you an instance which I think proves this. In the sixties I gave four lectures at the New School, and she came and sat in the audience at all of them and took a certain amount of bows and credits. The marriage ended after a gradual erosion of affection and compatibility. It took me a long time to realize it wasn't salvageable. And it wasn't only loyalty in my psyche — I took great pride in the marriage. I thought this was the best marriage I'd ever heard anything about. I kept thinking: somehow I'll work it out, pull it off. It was a great shock to my pride. It's too bad Prossy didn't fall for somebody at the time I left, but somewhere in her psyche, with all the trauma the case represented, the rope she clung to was: loyal wife."

Al got his new job, after a year of looking around, through Edith Levy, a woman who was working at the New School, to whom he happened to mention that he was out of work. Edith called up a smart big-time printer named Sam Chernoble, a local Republican committeeman, who hired Al on the spot, taught him the printing business, and put him to work in a stationery-and-printing shop he owned, called Davison-Bluth, on Fifth Avenue between 19th and 20th streets.

Sam Chernoble said Al was a good student and picked up the business quickly. Sam only had to explain things to Al once. "Intelligence is intelligence," Sam said. "With Alger Hiss's brains and my brawn — we could have gone places. It's a business where you can make business by helping your customers. Your service is helping keep their own operations in good order. You walk around an office, and look around, and you can tell them, 'You know, you'd better reorder those letterheads now. You've only got a hundred left and it'll take a couple weeks to print them.'" Al got on the phone and pounded the pavement and lined up about a hundred and fifty accounts — firms who needed stationery, brochures, catalogues, book jackets, invoices, posters, announcements, form letters. "Donie asked me, 'How can you be a salesman?' but I liked it. My technique was I call up a place and say, 'I'm Alger Hiss.' 'Alger *who?*' 'Alger Hiss. I'm a printing salesman now and I'd like to come in and discuss it.' They didn't always give me business, but they always saw me when I said 'Alger Hiss.'" An early customer — the account didn't work out — had Andy Warhol as a graphics designer. This was a fancy leather business that kept a live alligator in an aquarium in the foyer of the office. Andy wanted some super-fancy stationery. Al explained it wouldn't turn out looking like what Andy had in mind. Andy said Al wasn't trying hard enough.

These days Al *is* Davison-Bluth — Sam sold the business in 1965 to another printer, S. Novick, and everyone else in D-B subsequently went on to other things. Al now works at a desk in the Novick offices on the second floor of the old Puck Building, once home of *Puck, The Comic Weekly,* at the corner of Houston and Lafayette. There's a statue of

Mr. Puck over the front door — a cherub in a top hat who's holding a pen and looking at himself in a mirror. You can see maybe an inch of green blotter at the front of Al's desk. The rest of the desk is covered with at least nine three-to-six-inch-high piles of letters, books, orders, newspapers, and notes, with a paperweight or pipe on top of each.

Al liked to write down notes in his engagement calendar about things that caught his eye — an interesting-looking building or an out-of-the-way place — as he walked up and down New York and made his rounds servicing his accounts. His '63 calendar has a long list — "iron front balustrade 6th Avenue and 20th Street, Talleyrand plaque 6th and Spring, Pharmacie Francaise 10th Ave., Spanish and Portuguese Cemetery, 11th and 6th," etc. He liked to take me for walks and point out amazing things I'd never noticed. Under MEMORANDA in the '63 calendar he wrote down, "So deep was the ignorance and credulity of the times that the most absurd of fables was received with equal reverence in Greece and in France . . . the emperors and the Romans were incapable of discerning a forgery that subverted their rights and freedom . . .' Gibbon vol 3 pp 25–27 Mod. Lib. Giant ed. re the decretals and donation of Constantine — forged in 8th Cent., not fully discredited until the end of 18th, according to Allan Nevins, Gateway to History, pp. 125/6."

This was followed by: "11/23/63 NY *Times* Joey Giardello, banned in N.Y. since 1956 for associating with undesirables, said 'What else is there besides undesirables?' "

While I was at Harvard Al enjoyed engaging me via letter in discussions about moral, personal, and cultural values. Occasionally he wrote me about myself. August 1961: "Apart from wholesome occasional outbursts of temper, you certainly have been a controlled one — the trouble with your tight control is that you acquire painful concepts that would dissipate with airing. Of course you feel distressed and an-

noyed with yourself that you haven't got much enjoyment out
of most of the courses and so haven't been able to put out
much. That, my modest son, is primarily the fault of the
college curriculum. I would expect that from now on and
especially in graduate work you will find things quite different.
Many have, including your pa. Surely the concentration on
high marks at Dalton was part of the 'stiff upper lip' pattern,
the pressure to be an example you felt was forced on you as
a result of my case. If you relax you not only won't torment
yourself but, as you get further away from the false, forced-
draft, over-dutiful, stiff-upper-lip whip within, you'll be able,
when you really want to, to pull off the tour de force you
used to glory (over glory?) in. Any comments or rebuttal will
be carefully considered." October 1961: "I talked to Prossy
last Wednesday. She flatly refused to agree to a divorce. I've
told her I expect her to change her view and will continue to
ask for a divorce. I still feel, despite our talk (i.e., yours and
mine), that the details of the collapse of Prossy's and my
relations are for her and me alone, except — so far as I'm
concerned — some elements may have to be gone into because of my relations to you and yours to me. So I'll say no
more of this meeting just now."

Well, that was then. Al also sent me a five-page "Essay on
Basic Values of a Man of Culture" he sat down and wrote —
I found it the other day. The conclusion of the essay goes:
"It is no doubt from some points of view a dispiriting time
for an artist or even for a connoisseur of the arts. But, more
broadly viewed, the artist can be buoyed — and the connoisseur also — by his capacity for sensing in advance the evolving
universal values. Artists have in this respect always been in
advance of their times. Most artists have struggled successfully in adverse circumstances and have had the validity of
their vision recognized only after long obscurity, sometimes
even after their deaths." When I read this essay the other

day — and I probably never read it when he sent it to me — I thought: Al is talking about himself here, and as an artist. You know, I think he really wanted to stay in art school back there after he left Powder Point. *Art* school, I never thought of that before; not law school. What do you know? I'll have to think about that.

Al's name got back in the papers in 1970 when the American Civil Liberties Union sued the government to get him his State Department pension of sixty-one dollars a month. He hadn't been getting it because when he got out of the jug scores of congressmen introduced bills to deny him the dough. The result was an act that did just this, the so-called Hiss Act. The chief judge in the case, Roger Robb, a Nixon appointee, who had been the prosecutor in the Oppenheimer case, eventually ruled the bill was ridiculously unconstitutional, and Al took a short trip to Europe on the accumulated back pension, although he and the ACLU lawyer were a little disappointed at not being able to take the case to the Supreme Court — Al wanted vindication at the highest level and Sandy Rosen loves to go to the Supreme Court. But Solicitor General Erwin Griswold, our old friend Whoppo, wouldn't appeal Robb's decision. In 1974, a move in Congress to deny recently ex-President Nixon his federal pension was quashed because of the Robb ruling in the Hiss case. Three years ago, when Al saw that Dick Nixon was well on his way to becoming an ex-President, he decided that instead of working on a book about the New Deal, he would take a shot at pressing for total vindication. He's now teamed up with Edith Tiger, the director of the Emergency Civil Liberties Committee, the Avis of the civil liberties' organizations; Bill Reuben, the encyclopedia of the Hiss Case who walks like a man, a journalist who's compiled an 800-page unfinished dossier on Chambers; and Randy Walster, a young lady lawyer in Leonard Boudin's office. This combo last year got access to the never-before-seen-except-by-Dick Nixon Pumpkin Papers microfilms — the ones that reproduce the Navy Department memos about the color of fire extinguishers, etc. — and they expect to be ready to go into court to challenge the verdict in *United States* v. *Alger Hiss* this year. In 1975, on a day that happened to be my thirty-fourth birthday, Al was readmitted to the bar in Massachusetts. His first appearance before the House Committee in 1948 came on my seventh birthday.

Counselor Alger Hiss spends less time being Davison-Bluth than he used to — he's working on his case and raising money for it and also paying off the balance of his legal fees in Massachusetts on the college lecture circuit — Michigan State, West Texas State, Duke, Bard, and Boston University. Mrs. Tillie Novick, his boss in the printing business, says, "When your dad's away, it's unfortunate for the business, because everything stops. None of his clients will deal with anyone else. They all say, 'We'll wait for Al.' He always gives the customer every advantage in price, which is uncommon in this business. I think he thinks of himself last — I've often kidded him about it. Some customers are demanding, and I've told him he could at least get the satisfaction of a slightly higher commission. He's a tremendous, tremendous idealist. I've often talked with your father about the demands, innuendoes, the falsehoods, the lies you meet in this business. He never loses his cool. Never, never, but never. Now we're happy he doesn't have so much time for us because things are so well for him — in the last two years age has washed away from him. I've been working fifty years, in this business forty years. My mother wanted me to be a schoolteacher, but I had to work and I've never regretted it, because exposure to the world gives you a chance to become a much more honest or honorable person."

Bill Karson, a Novick salesman and a CCNY grad in economics who was blind from birth, says, "The first conversation

I had with Alger was about buying toilet paper for one of our accounts. I hung up and said, 'I can't believe it — I've just had a conversation with Alger Hiss about toilet paper!' What happens with Alger Hiss when he's in, there isn't a person who doesn't stop by his desk and want to talk to him. I think he enjoys talking about anything — sometimes he and I make prognostications. In a nutshell, he thinks the situation is going to get worse before it gets better. He's not even sure about the next generation. But it will very definitely turn around. I say, 'There may not be a world when things get around to turning around.' He says, 'There's got to be a world, there always has been.' I think he's cheered me up sometimes — he always calls me a pessimist. I tell him 'You're too goddamn easygoing.' I spotted that Weinstein two years ago — saw him on television and something rubbed the wrong way. Alger said, 'He's all right, he's making a career, he's climbing.' I said, 'Climbing on your back.' Now he says, 'You were right, Bill.' "

Kelly Carnahan, the salesman with the elegant, slightly curled mustache and red bow tie who sits at the desk facing Al's: "We blow smoke at each other. He's an amazing man — the inner calmness gets through to everybody. Is he a good salesman? He said, 'I don't have customers, I have friends.' He did say once that when he finally loses his temper and decides to yell, no one seems to notice because everyone yells here — which I can relate to. I'm the person who opens his mail when he's not here. Sometimes he shows it to me. Really, after the amount of time that's passed, you would've thought the crank letters would've dwindled off. Did he show you that long single-spaced one about the Episcopalian-Communist plot that ended up 'If you don't send money, I won't correspond with you?' I think he thoroughly enjoys not talking politics. He's a sounding board. Anyone who has an opinion insists on telling him. He saves his *New States-*

man crossword puzzles for me. I save for him my Manchester *Guardians*, which I don't think he ever reads, but he dutifully glances at them."

Ben Friedman, chief purchasing officer, sits two desks away from Al and likes to chew a small cigar and a toothpick at the same time: "I kid around with him — ask him 'Where have you been, you've been gone so long? Where are you going? Take me with you!' He talks about that young cousin of his, Mike Hiss, the racing car driver. He's too easygoing. If they did that to me, I'd kill somebody."

Marvin Pollock, chief of letter press in the shop: "The women in the diner he eats in — Buffa's — are all crazy about him."

Joe Behar, photo offset press foreman: "When we heard he was coming here we had our doubts about how a person like that would act. We didn't know what to expect, because you don't know a man till you work with him. The first time we heard that a high-up political type person was coming to work here, Mr. Kaplan came in and said — he wouldn't tell us the name — 'I'll give you a hint. He hates Richard Nixon.' And I came out with 'Whittaker Chambers!' I didn't know anything about the case. Then when I heard it was Al I went out and read the books. As far as I'm concerned, when we first met, within a week I felt as if I'd known him a really long time. More than a week. Now he's almost a member of my family. He's understanding, mostly. There are a lot of intangibles in printing. He came in with a couple of rough jobs right at the beginning — a lot of these process jobs run into certain problems. I could tell him about the problems, and he was able to convince the customers we did a good job. The other thing I liked about him — with a man that dignified, we could use our language, rather than what we imagined to be his language. We had been worried about that, too, but after the first week we knew we had no problems."

Paul Battista used to be Novick's "Stripper" — the most highly skilled craftsman in any offset shop, who has to position and correct every negative to the finest fraction of an inch — until he left a couple of years ago to open his own printing plant in Yonkers. Paul Battista told me recently: "For the short space of time that Mr. Hiss has been in this field, I would say that he has caught on to it pretty good."

When Al's news dealer introduced Al to his wife, she said, "Glad to know you. You sure sold a lot of papers, Mr. Hiss."

At one point when I was writing this book, Al was eclipsed in the papers by Arlene Hiss, separated wife of Mike Hiss, who wants to be the first woman to drive in the Indy 500. There was only a small item about Al — Nelson Rockefeller had told a private gathering of big-time Republican backers in Atlanta that a woman who worked for Scoop Jackson was a former avowed Communist who had once been on Alger Hiss's staff at San Francisco.

The last time I was talking to Al he suddenly said: "I'm surprised I never mentioned this, but I just thought of it. It used to wake me up laughing in the middle of the night about it. Just after I started working at the Department of Justice — must have been shortly after I met Chambers, actually — and new colleagues from the SG's office were coming over to the house more often than the Triple A crowd like Louis Bean, the great statistician, Gardner Means, and Dr. Mordecai Ezekiel, one of the brain trusters of production control, our maid, Martha Pope, wonderful woman, said one night, 'Mr. Hiss, where are all those Communists who used to come here so often? Have you seen 'em around?'

" 'Communists?'

" 'Mr. Ezekiel, Mr. Bean. Ecommunists — isn't that the word?' "